To: Nick, ("Deep TecNo")

Great to dive with you.

Cheers,

Martyn Farr, August 2006.

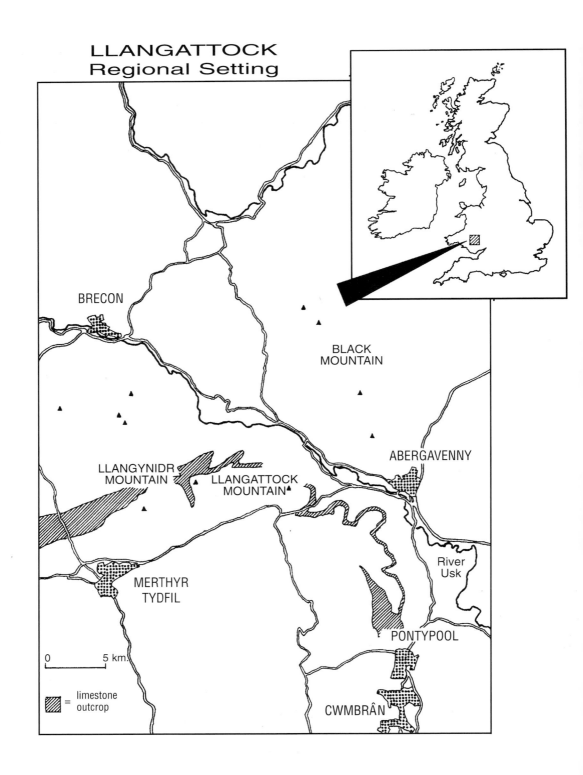

LLANGATTOCK
Regional Setting

BRECON

BLACK
MOUNTAIN

ABERGAVENNY

LLANGYNIDR
MOUNTAIN

LLANGATTOCK
MOUNTAIN

River
Usk

MERTHYR
TYDFIL

PONTYPOOL

CWMBRÂN

0   5 km

= limestone
outcrop

DARKWORLD

The Secrets of Llangattock Mountain

Martyn Farr

First Impression—1997

ISBN 1 85902 501 3 (hardback)
ISBN 1 85902 595 1 (softback)

Printed in Wales at
Gomer Press, Llandysul, Ceredigion

To Jane
The light of my life
To thank you for making it all possible

ACKNOWLEDGEMENTS

It has taken over ten years to complete *Darkworld* and during this period I have received a considerable amount of help from many people.

For assistance in the research stage, I should particularly like to thank all those who spared many hours and helped set the historical background into perspective: Brian Price, the late Mel Davies, Paul Hartwright, Kingsley Hawkins, Paul Hayward, David Leitch, Dr Harold Lord, the late Ken Pearce and Tony Oldham. I am indebted to John Van Laun for information relating to the industrial history of the area.

The diary entries of Clive Gardener, Bill Gascoine and Ann Franklin have been extremely useful, whilst conversations with Steve Pedrazzoli, Clive Westlake, Mike Wooding, Pete Cousins, John Cooper and many others have all served to complete the picture of activities at Llangattock.

For the exellent mapwork, I am deeply grateful to Dave Ramsey and Pete Fowler. For the loan of photographs, I am particularly indebted to Brian Price, William Maxwell, Dr Harold Lord, Karl Martin, John Dyer, Stewart Baggs and Gavin Newman. I must also acknowledge the photographic assistance offered by my long-suffering caving companions: Hugh Durban, Nick Geh, Steve Pedrazzoli, Stewart Baggs and Pete Fowler. Likewise, for his work in the production of prints, and for a wealth of invaluable, constructive criticism relating to the text I am particularly indebted to my friend Chris Howes.

Finally, I am eternally indebted to Jane for her assistance with local research, patient understanding, encouragement and support.

LLANGATTOCK AND THE ESCARPMENT

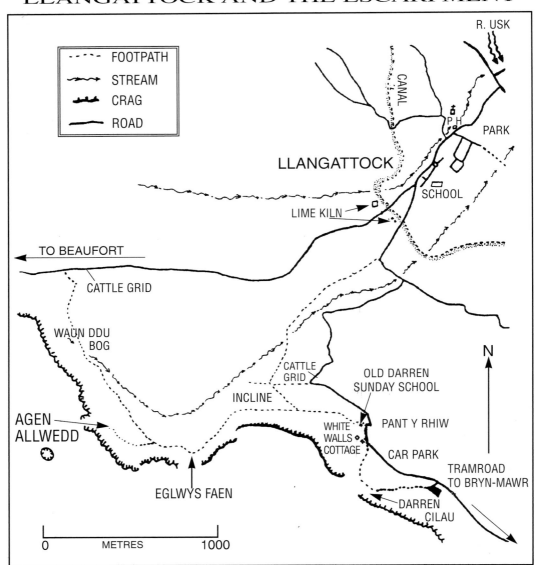

FOOTPATH
STREAM
CRAG
ROAD

R. USK

CANAL

P H

PARK

LLANGATTOCK

SCHOOL

LIME KILN

TO BEAUFORT

CATTLE GRID

WAUN DDU BOG

CATTLE GRID

OLD DARREN SUNDAY SCHOOL

INCLINE

AGEN ALLWEDD

PANT Y RHIW

WHITE WALLS COTTAGE

CAR PARK

TRAMROAD TO BRYN-MAWR

EGLWYS FAEN

DARREN CILAU

N

0   METRES   1000

CONTENTS

An artist's impression of Llangattock in 1795. Llangattock House in the foreground. From *A Picturesque Guide Through Wales and the Marches* by James Baker, 1795.

Llangattock Mountain from above Crickhowell.

Llangattock
Mystery and Legend; Curiosities and Caves

In the south-east corner of the Brecon Beacons National Park the river Usk quietly winds its way between the high plateau of the Black Mountains and a rugged, imposing escarpment overshadowing the small town of Crickhowell. This is an area of great beauty and considerable charm; one of the principal gateways to Wales. Standing stones, burial chambers and long abandoned hill-forts lie scattered in a chequered landscape of lush water meadows, rough grazing and patchy woodland. Discreet and mysterious, these relics of a bygone age are but a few of the many interesting features of this part of South Powys. Equally intriguing are the natural wonders of Craig y Cilau Nature Reserve and Mynydd Llangatwg (Llangattock Mountain).

Craig y Cilau Nature Reserve, a National Nature Reserve, occupies a secluded, 157 acre site high above the village of Llangattock. This north-facing, amphitheatre-like area is in every sense a most unusual feature. It is treasured not only for its wealth of rare flora and fauna but also for a system of caves quite unlike any other in the British Isles, or indeed the world.

Surmounting the crags, which appear to ring the upper tier of the precipitous escarpment and which largely enclose the reserve, lies a broad expanse of bleak moorland. This is the domain of grouse, curlew and skylark; a windswept boggy moor of cottongrass, heather and bilberry. Ancient burial mounds dating to the Bronze Age stand pimple-like above the low summit of Mynydd Pen-cyrn, beyond which the surface gradually dips away towards the heartland of industrial South Wales. This gently undulating plateau is pock-marked by thousands of circular cone-shaped depressions. From the air the surface of Llangattock Mountain and the adjoining upland of Mynydd Llangynidr appears almost lunar-like, presenting a rash of mysterious craters; steep-sided holes in the ground testifying to the one time existence of deep, inaccessible chambers or cavities, many of which have long since succumbed to catastrophic roof failure. These craters exhibit no regular pattern and, surprisingly, few caves can be entered through the chaotic jumble of boulders to be found at their base.

Here and there small streams issue from peat bogs but all are quickly engulfed, their waters 'lost' to some unknown subterranean course. The indications are clear: somewhere deep beneath the surface there lies an extensive network of caves stretching in a wide band to both east and west.

The caves at Llangattock have been known to locals for many hundreds of years. The best known is situated about a mile above the village, in an isolated angle of the escarpment, half way up the mountainside. Here in a prominent 'dry valley' or ravine several interconnecting entrances, known locally as Eglwys Faen—the Stone Church—are to be found.

Unlike the famous caves of England, no great river drains from or into Llangattock Mountain. It is not surprising, therefore, that in historical times early travellers through South Wales were attracted to a better known cave, about 20 miles to the west, called Porth yr Ogof (Gateway to the Cave) or, sometimes, the White Horse Caves. Here, the river Mellte, part of the headwaters of the river Neath, disappears into a most impressive entrance over 10 metres wide and three metres high. For centuries, adventurous or eccentric travellers would visit the site and many awe-inspiring accounts of underground explorations subsequently appeared in print, recounting the experiences of visitors who had toured the 'vasty chambers wreathed in cloudy vapours' by the light of candles or flaring torches.

Apparently, Llangattock boasted no such wonders similar to those of Porth yr Ogof . . . but events would prove otherwise. A series of breakthroughs and associated scientific studies have revealed that the major caves beneath the mountain form part of a single, massive system—an extremely complex network rating as one of the longest in the world, still only partially explored and whose ultimate extent can only be imagined.

The Llangattock caves certainly have a colourful history but surprisingly little was actually written about them until the turn of the eighteenth century. In ages past the caves had to be approached on foot, directly from the valley. It was an arduous route; a steep boulder-strewn slope covered in a thicket of thorn and low scrub. To those with time at their disposal to appreciate the surroundings, this was a wildly beautiful place. High above the Usk valley there were fine views of the Norman settlement in Crickhowell, the Iron Age hill-fort on Table Mountain, north of the town, and the steep, windswept Black Mountains beyond.

It was during the eighteenth century that the great 'County Chronicles' made their appearance for the first time—a history of people and places in the various shires across the country. The *History of the County of Brecknock* (today part of the county of Powys) was compiled by Theophilus Jones and published in September 1805. Jones paints an exquisite picture of one particular cave:

> One of them is called Eglwys Faen, the stone church, or church of or in the rock; the entrance into it is low and troublesome, but upon advancing further, by the assistance of torch or candle light, a spacious vaulted room is discovered, from the roof and sides of which stalactites are everywhere pendent, some of them clear, like icicles, while in others the calcareous matter is arrested and petrified in the falling, and if the light be very strong they exhibit a brilliant display of natural gems. This church, which was also occasionally a place of concealment, or retreat from an enemy, as the name Darren y cil-le imports, is ninety yards long, thirty six wide and thirty feet high, and on the right and left are several lofty winding passages leading into other openings, not so large or high, until at last the rock drops so low that they cannot be further explored.

This insight to the area is particularly valuable to both historian and caver alike. It was written in the days before any major tramroads had been laid, before any widespread quarrying had disfigured the escarpment. It clearly implies that there were several caves on the mountainside and that the Main Chamber of Eglwys Faen was originally well decorated with rock formations. Sadly, most of the latter have since been broken and destroyed. Just where the other caves were to be found is unknown.

Delving further into the history and folklore of the mountain provides a yet more colourful picture. As early as 1538 a survey of the Beaufort Estate refers to Llangattock Mountain as 'Cille Lan' or the 'Hill of Refuge' a place-name element still preserved in the names of 'Ciliau' and 'Penciliau' farms adjacent to the Beaufort-Llangattock road. The inference again is clear; that through the ages the caves have afforded shelter to fugitives.

By far the most interesting aspect of this early history relates to the naming of Eglwys Faen, 'the stone church', itself. As Theophilus Jones records, the name was in use well before 1800. Welsh place-names are often descriptive, frequently relating to some geographical feature nearby. Certainly there was no man-made church anywhere in the vicinity. Could the name have been given to describe the cavern's size and grandeur, similar to 'Cathedral Cave', a recent description of one show cave in the upper Swansea valley? Might some early saint or religious hermit have used the site for solitary devotions? Neither can be dismissed but learned authorities argue that the name suggests that the cave provided a meeting-place during times of religious persecution.

Two independent pieces of documentary evidence support this theory. In the mid 1640s, in the wake of the Civil War, Oliver Cromwell completely overturned the established political and religious order in Britain and replaced it with a harsh Puritan regime. In conservative, Royalist areas such as Wales these changes were far from popular. The rector of Llangattock, Matthew Herbert, like many others up and down the country, was ejected from his church in 1645 and thrown upon the mercy of his friends. His successor, Matthew Williams, was not liked by the majority of the population and records show that derogatory epithets were applied to itinerant preachers who replaced the ejected clergy. Llangattock preachers were referred to as 'iterates' and Edward Dafydd of Margam, for example, described others as 'blind ones who commit grievous frauds'. The peasant ballad writers of the time referred with regret to '. . . the learned Doctor who has been set aside', and '. . . the impudent churls who roar and bellow in the market place'.

Despite his ejection Herbert, who was well respected locally, continued to preach, apparently until 1655. His sermons, of necessity, would have been delivered in secret, presumably well away from the village.

A second piece of evidence suggests that Eglwys Faen was, in fact, the site where the secret services were held. Henry Vaughan (1621-95), one of the great Metaphysical Poets, studied under Matthew Herbert in Llangattock for six years prior to the Civil War. Born to a well-to-do local family (his grave lies in Llansanffraed churchyard, near Tal-y-bont), Vaughan was given the education of a gentleman and regarded Herbert's tuition with great respect. While the poet's later publications are in English, it is likely that he grew up speaking Welsh, and whilst staying with Herbert he would have gained a detailed knowledge of the area and its legends. His poetry, written during the Cromwellian era, depicts a Puritan republican regime which, in his opinion represented a wilderness, both religious and political.

In Vaughan's work references to caves are frequent:

> As he that in some Caves thick damp
>> Lockt from light,
> Fixeth a solitary lamp,
>> To brave the night
> And walking from his Sun, when past
>> That glim'ring Ray
> Cuts through the heavy mists in haste
>> Back to his day.

At no point does Henry Vaughan refer to Eglwys Faen by name but the inference in 'Jacobs Pillow, and Pillar' in his volume entitled *Poems* is certainly worthy of careful scrutiny. The poem begins thus:

> I see the Temple in thy Pillar rear'd,
> And that dread glory, which thy children fear'd . . .

Could this be a reference to the huge pillar of rock in which is situated Eglwys Faen, the dark cave which, in ages past, was reputed to lead down to Hell? The poem continues:

> This little Goshen, in the midst of night,
> And Satans seat, in all her Coasts hath light,
> Yea Bethel shall have Tithes (saith Israels stone)
> And vows and visions, though her foes crye, None.
> Thus is the solemn temple sunk agen
> Into a Pillar, and conceal'd from men.

Vaughan had an intimate knowledge of the Bible and frequently used the people, places and themes contained therein within his own works. In this instance, Jacob's Dream provided the framework and in Genesis Goshen is referred to as 'a place where God's chosen people can be safe, where the surrounding land is hostile'.

It seems probable, therefore, that religious services were held in this cave during Cromwell's era, a cavern subsequently named Eglwys Faen.

A considerable amount of later folklore also relates to the cave. Quite apart from a legend recalling the adventures of a dog which is supposed to have entered the cave and 'come out at Newport with all the hair scraped off its back', Eglwys Faen has been the focus of several other interesting stories. For example, in the early twentieth century the late Dr Morgan MD and others of the Crickhowell area are said to have heard a ghost choir singing in the cave on Midsummer's Eve. Another local resident recalls being taken to the cave by his mother in about 1910, when he was suffering from whooping cough. She then proceeded to swing him round and round in the Main Chamber, in an attempt to drive the cough out of his system!

*   *   *

When Theophilus Jones was in the process of completing his *History of the County of Brecknock* (1805) great changes were about to have a major impact on the area, particularly on the limestone escarpment at Llangattock.

By an Act of Parliament passed in 1793 permission was granted to construct a canal, together with a network of 'feeder' tramroads, from Newport to Brecon, the primary purpose of which was to serve the growing trade in coal. The section from Newport to Gilwern was opened in 1795, and extended to Llangattock in the summer of 1797. Collieries at the head of the Clydach valley, near Bryn-mawr, expanded rapidly. The canal company quickly realised that, quite apart from coal, there was increasing demand for limestone, initially in the form of lime, to be sold as fertilizer. A local source of stone was needed.

And so quarrying began. By 1815 the solitude of Llangattock had been broken. The desolate hillside rang to the reverberating echo of iron on rock. With picks and spades, the thin covering of soil was stripped aside and with the aid of bar and sledgehammer, the precious limestone rock was prized free.

A coal barge on the Newport-Brecon canal early in the twentieth century.

(Photo: *Museum of Welsh Life*)

Craig y Cilau Nature Reserve. The old tramroad (footpath) leads to Eglwys Faen, situated in the prominent bluff immediately beyond the first long shadow (left of frame). The tramroad then follows the contours for 500 metres to Ogof Agen Allwedd, situated to the left of the prominent scree slope, at the far right of the picture.

Scores of men toiled away from early morning to dusk laying tramroads to serve an ever growing number of workings, slowly establishing a network of lines around the side of the mountain. Initially, the limestone was taken to the kilns on the canal bank far below but, later, to the spreading industrial complex at Nant-y-glo and Beaufort. The Industrial Revolution had come to Wales.

From the quarry workings contouring the side of Llangattock Mountain, more and more rock was extracted, and in the process many more caves were uncovered from beneath the scanty layer of soil and scree. The entrances to places which cavers today

The old tramroad leading to Eglwys Faen, showing holes drilled into the stone sleepers. The metal pins which these once contained held the iron rails in position.

refer to as Pen Eryr, Darren Cilau and Agen Allwedd were revealed. On the other side of the mountain, in the Clydach gorge, quarrying operations gave access to the Craig a Ffynnon, or Rock and Fountain, cave system. Wherever limestone was freely available, the rock was either being worked or new quarries were contemplated.

The caves were also of interest to the quarrymen. As in ages past they provided convenient shelter from the elements and the once abundant inscriptions—names, dates and place of residence—on the walls of Eglwys Faen, for instance, give clear evidence that occasionally the more curious workers sometimes explored deep into the passageways, well beyond the glimmering light of the entrance. Although several examples of graffiti dating back to the 1830s can still be found, sadly the majority have been totally defaced during the second half of the twentieth century.

The changes wrought upon the hillside above Llangattock are worthy of elaboration. For hundreds of years small-scale lime burning, fuelled by a ready source of charcoal, had taken place on the mountain. In 1815, a row of kilns was erected on the canal bank at Llangattock, and limestone was transported to the furnaces via a half-mile long tramroad and two steep inclines. Getting the rock out of the quarries and down to the valley below was not easy! The inauguration of the steep incline appears to have been something of a disaster and a letter, dated 3 June 1815, from the general manager of this development to his principals at Clydach Colliery is of interest:

> As for the state of the Llangattock Road I am sorry to have to say that we went very ill by defects in the machinery chains &c. caused a breakage of some of the Trams but at present it begins to work very well. The principal injury done was in breaking Tram Wheels there is but One Tram but what can be imiatly fitted up Eight was the number injured Two of them since fitted up and only waiting for Wheels when we shall again have the all on Works Hoping there will be no more such Accidents but it is mostly the Case in all new Erections not to go so well at the Commencement every thing being strange the principal Thing wanting is a stock of Lime Stone as being no Stock anywhere when the Road was completed and all the Kilns on fire.

Initially, virtually all the limestone was transported to Llangattock for burning. However, on the other side of the mountain, ironworking had also commenced. Furnaces had been erected in the 1790s at Nant-y-glo, near Bryn-mawr, but it was not until the Bailey family took over the concern in 1811 that the enterprise flourished. Considerable quantities of limestone were now required for fluxing and as a consequence a tramroad was laid in the direction of Llangattock. Quarrying slowly began to extend westwards. A line of excavations began to ring the mountain.

Quite apart from all the raw materials required in the production of iron, serious consideration had to be given to the question of outlets. Initially, iron and coal was taken via the tramroads of the Clydach valley to the wharfs at Gilwern, but this route was supplemented in 1831 when, by a major feat of engineering, a five-mile tramroad (today the scenic metalled road which passes the entrance to Bryn-mawr

Secondary School and Hafod Farm) left Bryn-mawr, gracefully contouring the mountain at the 350 metre (1150 feet) level. This connected with the inclines previously constructed on the mountainside above Llangattock. Iron, but more especially coal, made its way along the tramroad in a westerly direction while limestone and timber, for use in the collieries, travelled east. Sometime shortly after 1840, *Cymro*, a steam locomotive—'Crawshay Bailey's Engine'—was brought into operation on this level section.

Quarrymens' houses sprang up on the Llangattock hillside, with the greatest concentration around the little hamlet at Pant y Rhiw (today the Cave Rescue Post is situated here, at White Walls Cottage, headquarters of the London-based Chelsea Spelaeological Society). But life was hard for the new immigrants who settled in the area. Cholera epidemics swept Bryn-mawr and adjoining communities, and at Llangattock industrial accidents took their toll, as the parish records show:

30 August 1850: John Santry, aged 10 years of the Workhouse—'killed by a quarry tram'.

14 August 1852: William Morgan, White Walls Cottage, Hillside, aged 33 years—'who lost his life by a fall of stone upon him at Llangattock quarries'.

June 1856: Maria Morgan, White Walls Cottage, Hillside, aged 11 years—'killed by the quarry steam engine going over her'.

10 September 1860: Edward Bevan, Pantyrhiw, Hillside, aged 60 years—'accidentally killed by a limestone tram'.

The population of Llangattock hillside continued to increase late into the 1880s. In response to this and the boom period in the quarries, five public houses sprang up along the tramroad leading to Bryn-mawr, including The Travellers Rest, next to White Walls Cottage; The Grouse, less than a kilometre away; and the Cymro, by the old sheep dip and present-day gas installation. Between 1850 and 1880 Darren Sunday School was erected, an immensely popular institution which at harvest thanksgiving frequently attracted quarry workers from as far afield as the villages of Llanelli and Clydach.

But time and technology was changing. By 1900 quarry fortunes were in decline. The Llangattock quarries were rapidly coming to the end of their useful working life, and about 1910 work ceased, although a small-scale lime-burning enterprise continued for some time. The two-way traffic along the tramroad, up and down the steep inclines, was to continue until 1911, when the whole operation finally fell into disrepair. People moved away, the five public houses and Darren Sunday School closed and by 1940 many buildings were in ruins.

Within the space of little more than 100 years Llangattock had witnessed the birth and death of a great industry. The quarries fell silent, grass and bracken clothed the spoil and the area regained its rural tranquility. But some of the changes wrought were indelible. A network of roads and tracks now rendered Llangattock hillside infinitely more accessible, particularly from Bryn-mawr. The old tramroad was soon a very popular spot for those residents of the industrial centres at the heads of the mining valleys with the time to take a few hours exercise and enjoy the breathtaking views, some of the finest in South Wales. And so it was that the Llangattock caves were to develop into something of a local tourist attraction. However, despite the fact that far more people knew of the caves after 1900, no serious cave exploration was to take place until after the Second World War.

Caving as a sport was slow to develop in Wales. In places like Derbyshire, for example, miners had explored many of the caves well before 1800, but here in the Pennines there was an ulterior motive, namely the quest for lead ore. It was not until the latter part of the nineteenth century that caves were explored for their own sake.

The birthplace of the sport of caving in the British Isles was to be the Yorkshire Dales, where, incidentally, a Frenchman, Edouard Martel, was credited with the first descent of the famous pothole, Gaping Gill, in 1895. Caving also developed, quite independently, in the Mendip Hills of Somerset and it was from this area that the first interest in Welsh caves was to arise. The so-called Dragon Group made a fleeting visit to Llangattock in October 1938 and all the easily accessible passages in Eglwys Faen were explored. The entire cave, or so it seemed, amounted to less than 300 metres in length. The group were not inspired by what they had found; Llangattock caves might be a local curiosity but it appeared that they were of no great regional importance.

The early pioneers, quite naturally, returned to the upper Neath and Swansea valleys where spectacular discoveries were anticipated. Out from the cavernous entrance to Dan yr Ogof, for example, flows one of the largest cave streams in the British Isles. By comparison the opportunities at Llangattock paled into insignificance.

Nevertheless Eglwys Faen did attract local attention. During holiday periods, curious youngsters occasionally walked or cycled to the cave from as far afield as Rhymney and other towns at the Heads of the Valleys. It was the summer of 1942 when one particular schoolboy from Ebbw Vale first became interested in the area. Brian Price had just moved to the town where his father had been appointed Postmaster. He was in his last term at the local county school when the local bank manager's son took him on a visit to Llangattock caves. Like his fellow pupils, Price knew nothing of caving as a sport and went

Brian Price, the first person to realise that vast systems lay undiscovered beneath Llangattock Mountain.

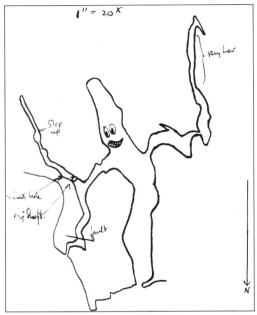

Brian Price's first sketch cave survey of Eglwys Faen, in 1946. The main entrance to the cave lies at the bottom of the 'figure'; a second entrance, the Oval entrance, lies to the left of the 'fault', while it is also possible to access the cave via the 'Big Shaft'—although this normally requires a ladder and lifeline.

Pock-marked craters. Llangynidr moors from the air

equipped on this and many other ventures clad in old clothes, and armed with candles or cycle lamps for illumination.

With a naturally inquisitive mind, Brian Price was more than an adventurous schoolboy. After discovering the area for the first time, he soon developed an interest in its history and, more especially, its caves. By the time he had entered his second year at Emmanuel College, Cambridge, Price had an accurately surveyed plan of Eglwys Faen framed and hanging on the wall of his digs. Drawn like a spectre, there was little doubt in his mind that there were many unanswered questions relating to the Llangattock hillside. What became of the small streams of water when they disappeared into the various blockages? How far did these caves extend?

During his vacations Price got to know the area well. He scoured the crags at Llangattock and explored the clefts and hidden ravines of the Clydach gorge. It was whilst he was at the University of Bristol, and on a term's teaching practice at Brynmawr County Grammar School, that his first concerted attempts were made to explore further the Llangattock caves. Together with some evacuee schoolboys billeted near Crickhowell he discovered two small unrecorded entrances half a mile beyond Eglwys Faen. Both entrances were impenetrable at this stage but both took a strong inward draught. On a weekend early in March 1946 a fire was ignited just inside the entrance to one of these in an attempt to see if the smoke emerged higher up the hillside. It didn't. Price was intrigued. He knew little about the circulation of air in caves but the evidence confronting him was sufficient to stir his imagination. As a continuous cloud of smoke billowed into the cave, and disappeared, Price quickly realised that there could be an extensive network of passages deep inside the mountain. They decided to name the hole after the shape of its entrance: Agen Allwedd (Cleft of a Key).

For the next two years Price taught in Westmorland and it was not until Christmas 1949 that anything more was done. By now Price had contacted the Rev. Cecil Cullingford (a renowned authority on caving), who was then headmaster of Monmouth School, and acquired from him the use of the old Sunday School at Pant y Rhiw, which by this time had become the Monmouth School's summer base for mountain expeditions.

The morning after they arrived, Christmas Eve, Price and his two young friends, Harold Hicken and David Seagrave, obtained a large crowbar and set off for the draughting hole. The large block which had previously prevented entry was quickly removed, then a further two. After half an hour the entrance was clear. A crawlway,

A group of Bryn-mawr scouts outside the entrance to Ogof Gam, 16 September 1950. *Back row, left to right*: Alan Williams, Derrick Williams. *Front row*: John Stanton (Bryn-mawr), Melvyn Williams, Ralph Tonsill.

(Photo: *Brian Price*)

Harold Hicken (left) and David 'Sally' Seagrave (right) outside the old Darren Sunday School at Pant y Rhiw on 2 January 1950.

(Photo: *Brian Price*)

hardly bigger than the opening to a badger sett, disappeared into the hillside. Agen Allwedd was a cave at last and henceforth named in the customary manner—the name preceded by 'Ogof', the Welsh word for 'cave'.

The pipe-like tunnel that confronted them was small and difficult to negotiate. Hicken squirmed his way in, quickly followed by the other two. Bones of rabbit and a badger's skull lay strewn along their path. The cave continued in much the same vein for 60 metres. They were then confronted with a real problem; they had reached an extremely intimidating squeeze. They named the spot Sally's Alley.

Over the next couple of days Price devised a method for passing this obstacle. Very simply, the route forward consisted of a tight body-sized tube—hardly more than two handspans in diameter—the floor of which was largely missing, and replaced by a deep fissure. Any attempt to squeeze along in this roof tube could result in the explorer slipping and becoming hopelessly wedged.

On the day after Boxing Day they began to drag large rocks into the cave and wedge them like key stones, or chock-stones, in the narrow section between the upper pipe and the floor. After several hours had elapsed they were tired from the stone hauling and distinctly chilled by the strong draught. They withdrew.

Another three days passed. 'An east wind was playing on the entrance and a very strong draught blew through the cave [into the mountain],' explained Price. 'This made matters very difficult. Candles could not be kept alight; even my acetylene lamp went out twice, and our torches could not be relied upon for a long excursion.'

The intimidating section was finally passed and, leaving Price on the outer side of Sally's Alley, the two young scouts made a reconnaissance beyond the squeeze. Within 50 metres they entered an altogether larger tunnel, and it was an extremely jubilant pair who returned about an hour later with tales of walking-sized passages continuing ever deeper into the mountain.

On 2 January 1950 the trio explored their new cave. Clambering over huge boulders and partially eroded sandbanks, they passed scores of bats deep in the slumber of hibernation. Some 450 metres from the entrance they reached a roof fall, where boulders and smaller debris were piled in a perilous, chaotic jumble for as far as the eye could see. Such blockages are common in caves. Here, it was seemingly impossible to progress further; to disturb the stability of the obstacle by selectively removing a rock could easily lead to disaster. Beneath the blockage—now known as the First Boulder Choke—the small stream gurgled away on its mysterious course. Two days previously cave explorers in the Swansea valley, the main centre of activity, had pooh-poohed the possibility of discovering an extensive cave system at Llangattock! But the trio's new cave, Aggy Aggy as it was affectionately nicknamed, had now been established as the longest system in Wales, east of the Neath valley!

Price soon mapped the passages in the new cave and formulated a number of theories concerning the direction of water flow and its eventual point of reappearance on the surface. Price postulated that Llangattock Mountain concealed an immense cave network, probably stretching far to the east, in the direction of the Clydach gorge, and for a considerable distance to the west—a system the equal of any in the British Isles.

* * *

Socially, the early 1950s was a period of change. The austerity of the post-war years was disappearing; an altogether brighter future lay in prospect. Outdoor clubs began to spring up the length and breadth of the country. More and more people were encouraged to explore the mountains and, to a lesser extent, the caves. For example, Hereford Caving Club was founded in 1951 and this, like many other clubs of the era, began life as a dual facetted organisation; an outdoor club with a very strong rambling element. Travel was still difficult at this time and the obvious advantage to be derived from such a club was that transport could be shared. Hereford Caving Club organised regular monthly trips and hired a coach for the purpose; cavers and ramblers, therefore, travelled together, a compatible arrangement that was to continue well into the 1960s.

Rather nearer to Llangattock a slightly different club sprang up in Pontypool. Here British Nylon Spinners Ltd (later I.C.I. Fibres) established a huge industrial complex which, in 1953, employed a workforce of about 5,500 people. And it was here that another caving organisation—a spelaeological society—was established. The club, which received financial support from British Nylon Spinners, went from strength to strength. Based relatively locally, the Spinners' was the most active group in the Llangattock area, and late in 1955 it was Eglwys Faen that captivated their attention. Early in 1956, following several months of excavation—lying flat out on their stomachs and clearing away just enough mud to allow them to wriggle forward—they broke into open passage, to more than double the known length of the cave.

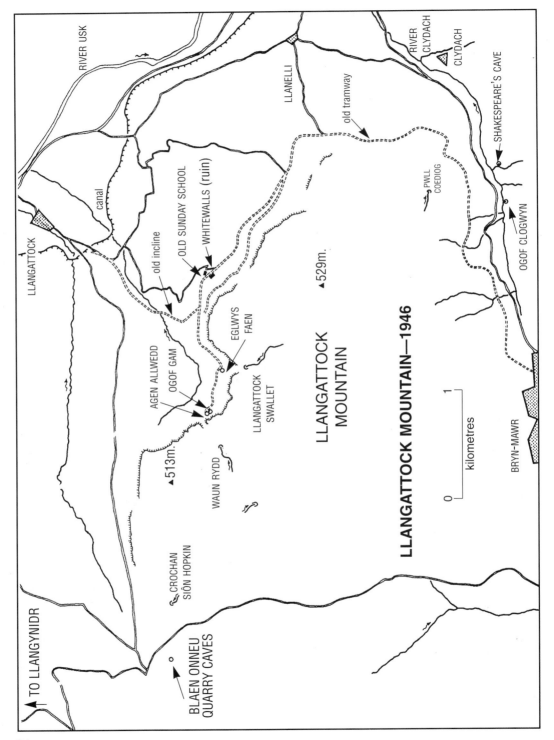

LLANGATTOCK MOUNTAIN—1946

LLANGATTOCK MOUNTAIN

RIVER USK

LLANELLI

old tramway

RIVER CLYDACH

CLYDACH

CLYDACH

SHAKESPEARE'S CAVE

PWLL COEDIOG

OGOF CLOGWYN

canal

OLD SUNDAY SCHOOL

WHITEWALLS (ruin)

old incline

▲529m.

AGEN ALLWEDD

OGOF GAM

EGLWYS FAEN

LLANGATTOCK SWALLET

LLANGATTOCK

BRYN-MAWR

▲513m.

WAUN RYDD

kilometres

0   1

CROCHAN SIÔN HOPKIN

TO LLANGYNIDR

BLAEN ONNEU QUARRY CAVES

Yet another club, which was to develop a very keen interest in the area, also emerged at this time. Members of Chelsea Spelaeological Society (the society was formally inaugurated in 1956) first visited the locality in the summer of 1955. Despite its relative remoteness—160 miles—Llangattock was nevertheless one of the nearest caving areas to London. The club soon realised the need for a permanent local base and in 1963 they purchased and subsequently developed the derelict White Walls Cottage, situated at the end of the now metalled tramroad from Bryn-mawr. Interest in Llangattock was gradually increasing. That the area held considerable potential was now no longer in doubt.

Karl Martin one of the founder members of the British Nylon Spinners Spelaeological Society, dressed for caving, *circa* 1952.

Eglwys Faen—the Main Passage illuminated by flash guns. Mindful of the approach path, the casual visitor can enter the substantial portal of the main entrance to savour the atmosphere of this scene.

Inscriptions on the walls of Eglwys Faen date back to 1836, and probably much earlier.

Over the years, considerable exploratory 'digging' has taken place in the various tunnels of Eglwys Faen in an attempt to enter the major series of passages which are postulated to lie beyond the known system. Clive Gardener negotiates an excavated section at the end of the Upper Series. Inexperienced cavers are advised to stay well clear of such areas!

Pure Luck: a Golden Era of Exploration

It was a dismal, grey autumnal morning as the coach drew up alongside the canal in Llangattock. The air was still and a thick blanket of cloud shrouded the escarpment. At the front of the bus Dave Kershaw stood and quietly rubbed his hands. 'This is it folks,' he exclaimed. 'We walk from here.'

Drowsy people yawned, stretched and looked at each other knowingly. Kershaw might well look bright and alert. He only lived just up the road in Llangynidr, whereas other members of the group had been on the road for over two and a half hours. The date was Sunday, 13 October 1957 and the occasion a routine monthly trip of the Hereford Caving Club.

With timetable and pick-up arranged, the rambling contingent quietly set off into the mist. Dave Kershaw was nominally in charge of caving operations for the day and he quickly briefed the dozen or so eagerly awaiting instructions. Most, like Kingsley Hawkins and Paul Hartwright, had never visited Llangattock, not to mention the caves on the hillside high above the village. They listened to Kershaw intently; he was the only one in the party who really knew the caves.

It was a long haul up the tramroad and inclines and there was plenty of time for reflection. Kingsley and Paul were fairly typical of the group. They had joined the club the previous year and their experience was limited to the organised monthly coach trips. By and large, these were all sporting 'tourist' trips, planned to follow the long established popular routes through the caves. This trip was no different. It was a gloomy start to a normal day's caving.

The tramroad led them on to Eglwys Faen where the various entrances were pointed out and Kershaw told them a little about the place. They were left in little doubt that it was well worth a visit, but not today.

'Agen Allwedd is less than half a mile away, straight along the path.'

Less than ten minutes later they had reached the small keyhole-shaped entrance to the cave. It wasn't very impressive. Sandwiches appeared, discussions took place and people got themselves organised.

By now they were all aware that the entrance section was going to be slow and awkward. It was decided that the first party should get started right away. Hopefully, this would minimize any hold-ups. The first party of six included Dave Kershaw, Kingsley Hawkins, Paul Hartwright and two Gloucester cavers, Paul Hayward and Tony Iles; others would follow at intervals.

Moving relatively smoothly, the six were soon out of earshot and well ahead of the rest. Nimbly shuffling and stooping through the gradually enlarging passage, spirits were high. Soon they were clambering over huge boulders covered in sand; it was now easygoing and straightforward. On reaching a junction, it was decided that two of the party would split off. Kershaw, Iles, Hayward and Hawkins would press ahead to the blockage where they would be joined by the other pair in the space of fifteen minutes or so. On reaching the 'final' blockage, it wasn't necessary to inform the newcomers in the party that they had arrived, for a prominent slab of rock spelt a clear warning. In bold, black, soot-stained letters someone had emblazoned the message 'DANGEROUS BOULDERS' with the aid of a carbide lamp.

'South Wales Caving Club had a dig here several years ago. Got in quite a distance, apparently; boulders all the way,' said Kershaw laconically.

The two Gloucester lads pricked up their ears. Hayward and Iles were well used to negotiating loose boulders in the old iron mines of the Forest of Dean—their home ground—and they decided to press on to assess the prospects for themselves. Hayward and Iles therefore took the lead and, peering into every nook and cranny, slowly moved forward into the choke.

It was now a matter of slithering flat out, ever so gently—up, over, down and along—between an endless succession of bouldery obstacles set against the line of a good, solid left-hand wall. To Hawkins, at the back of the column, it felt like being an ant on a trail around the inside of a bowl of sugar cubes.

'The constrictions, coupled with the still awe-inspiring slope of boulders on our right gave me plenty to think about,' recalls Hawkins. 'Once or twice it became necessary to remove our helmets and empty our pockets before forward progress could be made.'

After inching along this nightmarish route, hardly daring to breathe, the two Gloucester cavers entered a small chamber where the boulders appeared less densely packed, a point where cave explorers from the South Wales Caving Club had attempted to excavate down and to follow the passage at stream level. Hayward quickly came to the conclusion that this choice of route looked hopeless, but just a few metres short of the excavation he wriggled into an interesting looking lead along the line of the wall. He promptly squeezed forward, past a massive slab and, on encountering a steeply ascending mud slope, he carefully clambered on up for a further three or four metres. Suddenly, he emerged at the edge of a sizeable chamber.

'Hey, Tony, you'd better come up and see this . . . looks like a big chamber up here!'

In the space of a minute Iles had joined his friend and moments later an incredible sight appeared before their eyes. As they scrambled up an easy slope of hard packed mud and boulders, an enormous cavern opened before them, the like of which they had never seen before. This certainly wasn't the description they'd been given beforehand. They quickly returned to the choke and called down to their companions.

'Come on up; we're through to something big!'

'No, you can't be. South Wales have been digging it . . . there's no way on.'

Dave Kershaw was extremely sceptical; Hawkins didn't know what to believe. A few minutes later, however, the truth dawned and they were all beaming with delight. They had passed the choke, entered a huge cavern and they hadn't moved a single rock!

Paul Hartwright of Hereford Caving Club negotiates Salley's Alley, just a short distance from the original entrance of Ogof Agen Allwedd. Paul was a member of the party which made the dramatic discovery in the cave in October 1957.

Today Ogof Agen Allwedd is entered via the Ogof Gam entrance. In the interests of conservation and safety, the original route has been closed. A well trodden path leads to the entrance which is secured with a heavy steel gate, visible directly behind the two cavers, Martyn Farr (left) and Tony Donovan (right).

Directly inside Agen Allwedd is a logbook which records the details of every person entering, their intended journey and, most importantly, their expected time of exit.

Hardly daring to believe their luck, the four scrambled down a steep slope of dry muddy boulders and set off into the blackness, along what is now known as Main Passage.

'It was certainly the biggest passage I had ever seen,' recalls Hawkins. 'This was it, a big breakthrough and excitement was high as we hurried down the passage, looking anxiously for footprints. We found none, this was absolutely virgin territory—a marvellous feeling.'

Meanwhile Paul Hartwright and his companion had returned from their deviation. They knew that their friends had been heading directly for the choke at the end of the cave, so they quickly followed on. Having passed the danger warning and found everything silent, they wondered what to do. They knew the choke wasn't that long but the boulders appeared desperately loose, distinctly off-putting to the young explorers. Rather than push on they decided to sit and wait. As the cold gripped their bodies, they began to wonder if they had somehow passed their friends. Had they, for example, gone up another side tunnel some way back? The uncertainties persuaded Hartwright that they had better head slowly to the surface.

It was mid afternoon when they reached the entrance, and before they met any of the others in the party.

'Have you seen Dave and the others?'

'No, they haven't come back out yet.'

'That's very strange.'

Paul recalled the sequence of events.

There was no one keen enough to face the rigours of the entrance passage twice in one day and the main group wished to return to the bus in daylight. As a result, they all set off back along the track, curious but not unduly worried about the small party's whereabouts.

Darkness fell early. The driver was getting impatient and anxiety was slowly mounting. About an hour later lights appeared along the road. The missing group had arrived.

'Sorry we're late but you'll never believe this.'

Four grubby faces broke out in broad grins.

'We got through the choke! Loose . . . but huge passage beyond. It could be 25 metres wide and over 15 metres high in places . . . walking all the way . . . a kilometre or more. Bigger than any passage we've ever seen . . . Just couldn't believe it.'

'How did it end?'

'It didn't! Thought you'd be getting worried, so we turned round. It was huge, absolutely huge!'

Congratulations were heaped on the four, and they were bombarded by an endless succession of questions.

'Did you get back to the stream?'

'Didn't see it at all, but I think we heard it beneath the boulders at one spot.'

'The passage just went on . . . no idea in which direction. The floor was smooth, dry, hard-packed mud, but all cracked like the bed of a river or lake after a long drought. You had to watch the cracks, though. Some of them were two feet deep, and more than wide enough to take a misplaced boot. And there were crystals in some places, just growing out of the floor . . . 15 to 20 centimetres long . . . hundreds of them. It was absolutely fantastic!'

The details continued to pour out. Just where was this incredible passage heading? The speculation began. There was little doubt about it, this was unquestionably the most exciting day in the history of the club. The group were a-buzz all the way home. No one on the bus had ever found more than a few hundred metres of passage on previous occasions and now they had discovered one of the largest passages, possibly even one of the longest systems in Great Britain. What an incredible stroke of luck!

By March 1959 the system was established as the longest in the British Isles with a single entrance. Its length was in excess of 8 kilometres (5 miles) and it was abundantly clear that the cave might well extend for many kilometres in a downstream direction, and an even greater distance in the direction of Llangynidr Mountain. Agen Allwedd was now set amongst the longest caves in the world, the league at this stage being topped by the Holloch (Switzerland) which boasted over 72 kilometres (45 miles) of passageways.

Longer and longer trips were soon underway. Whereas in the early days of exploration, six or eight hours might have been the expected duration, a year after the breakthrough in Agen Allwedd some of the groups were involved in trips lasting 14 to 18 hours. For cavers such as Hawkins, who had to work on Saturday mornings, there were obvious difficulties in fitting such lengthy operations into the limited free time at their disposal.

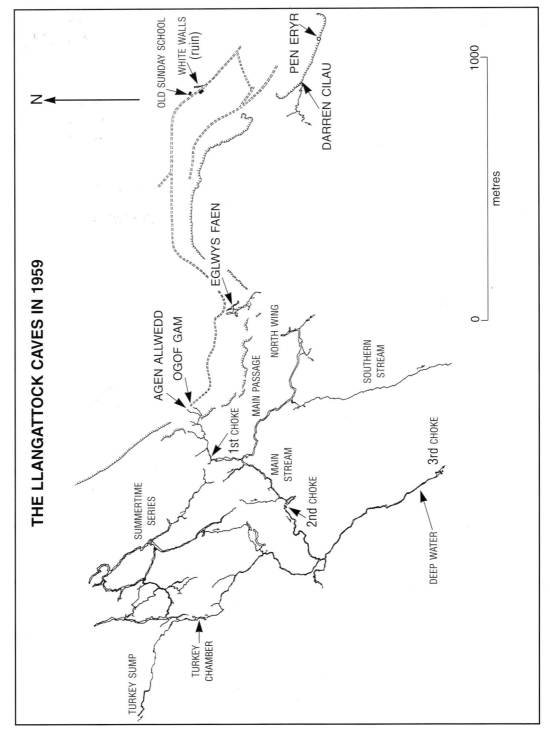

THE LLANGATTOCK CAVES IN 1959

N

OLD SUNDAY SCHOOL
WHITE WALLS (ruin)
PEN ERYR
DARREN CILAU
EGLWYS FAEN
AGEN ALLWEDD
OGOF GAM
1st CHOKE
MAIN PASSAGE
NORTH WING
SOUTHERN STREAM
MAIN STREAM
2nd CHOKE
3rd CHOKE
DEEP WATER
SUMMERTIME SERIES
TURKEY SUMP
TURKEY CHAMBER

0   metres   1000

To the Bitter End

News of the major developments at Llangattock spread quickly amongst cavers. This little known area was suddenly thrust into the limelight and all manner of people were soon keen to view the caves for themselves. They arrived from Mendip, Derbyshire and Yorkshire; cavers hardened by years of experience in the traditional, established caving regions. One of the foremost was Dr Harold Lord of the University College of North Wales, Bangor. Lord and his colleagues set about mapping the rapidly expanding network, quickly coming to the conclusion that an underground expedition was required. The route through the First Boulder Choke was enlarged and a vast quantity of gear was carried to their chosen camp site in Main Passage. An emergency telephone link was established to the surface, where a small support team sought to remedy any deficiencies that arose.

During Easter 1959 over ten whole days were spent underground, during which time they covered all the main passageways. Using a prismatic compass and steel tape, both forward and back bearings were taken at each survey station, thereby ensuring a high degree of accuracy. As a result of working very long hours 4.8 kilometres (3 miles) of mapped cave passageways were recorded in ten exercise books. What had previously been regarded as an almost impossible task, Lord and his small group had largely accomplished in one expedition.

Tents, cars and caravan gather on the tramroad in 1959, near Pant y Rhiw. From here the cavers walked the remaining half mile (750 metres) of tramroad, or rough footpath as it is today, to reach Eglwys Faen, and a further 500 metres to Ogof Agen Allwedd.

(Photo taken Sept. 1959 by BNSSS caver, John Dyer Ph.D.)

Cavers waiting their turn to enter Ogof Agen Allwedd, Sunday, 27th September 1959.

(Photo: *J. Dyer*)

In April 1959 the awesome caverns of the isolated Summertime Series had been discovered by the Hereford team and these, too, had to be included on the survey. Accordingly, an even more ambitious camp was organised for Easter 1960. Drawing upon their previous experience, Lord and his team decided to camp about two kilometres further from the surface. Porterage was again a major problem. On the '59 trip they carried everything into the cave via the tortuous, constricted 'keyhole' entrance but on this occasion it was decided to open a new, easier route into the system. The site in question was the neighbouring small cave, Ogof Gam.

A completely water-filled hollow at the end of the short, entrance passage had been passed on one previous occasion in 1951. Adopting advanced engineering and tunnelling skills the Ogof Gam route was 'opened' in 1960. This is now the normal point of access to the system, via a locked steel gate situated at the entrance. The original route was subsequently closed.

Early pioneers of the Pontypool-based BNSSS Mel Davies (left), and Ian Butterworth (right). The cavers demonstrate the equipment and clothing in use during the late 1950s: a cotton, one-piece oversuit, carbide lamp afixed to the front of a cardboard miners' helmet, reserve electric lighting, shoulder bag containing spare fuel and water for the lamp and essential food, etc. This photograph was taken in Ogof Pwll Swnd in west Wales.

(Photo: *J. Dyer*)

The huge main passage of Agen Allwedd, discovered in October 1957 by members of the Hereford Caving Club.

In the event, thirteen days were spent underground, and the eventual tally of passages surveyed amounted to 5.6 kilometres (3½ miles). The party resurfaced at 5.00 p.m. on 17 April 1960 after the longest venture of its type ever mounted in the British Isles—either before or since. Over 12.8 kilometres (8 miles) of passage had now been surveyed.

It was not until 1961 that cavers discovered where the water in the underground stream reappeared. The most likely spot appeared to be Ffynnon Gisfaen—the Gisfaen spring—located beneath the elevated section of the Heads of the Valleys Road at the head of the Clydach gorge. Yet another theory was that water might percolate all the way under the South Wales coalfield and resurge at a very large spring about 48 kilometres (30 miles) to the south, on the shores of the Bristol Channel.

As Ffynnon Gisfaen was used as a domestic water supply for the Bryn-mawr area, amateur hydrologist Mel Davies—a chemist at British Nylon Spinners—was careful not to cause pollution when he undertook his water-tracing experiments. Davies realised that it might take several days for the water to flow through the mountain. Since a visual siting could not be guaranteed, he relied upon 'detectors' set at various points along the length of the river. These strips of nylon yarn could be collected or replaced at regular intervals and inspected later for absorption of minute amounts of non-toxic dye. It was August 1961 when Davies finally proved that water from Agen Allwedd reappeared in the river Clydach, not at Gisfaen Pumping Station but about 80 metres upstream of the Devil's Bridge (directly below the site of the old Drum and Monkey public house). The water was found flowing up a flooded shaft—a hole known locally as Pwll y Cwm—in the centre of the river bed.

Following the publication of Harold Lord's survey in 1963, Agen Allwedd was shown to possess over 16 kilometres (10 miles) of passages, conclusively establishing it as the longest cave system in the British Isles and about the twelfth longest in the world. The majority of the 'easy' leads had largely been traced; the barriers that now confronted the explorers were formidable. The approaches yet to be tackled were the submerged sections at either end of Agen Allwedd and in the Clydach gorge.

The End and Beyond

Completely flooded passages, or 'sumps' as they are known to cavers, can be found in most caves. Without underwater breathing apparatus, considerable training and an iron nerve, sumps normally mark the end of exploration. Fewer than one percent of cavers embark upon cave diving for the simple reason that the activity is extremely dangerous, either by caving or diving standards. However, despite the dangers of venturing into the icy cold (7° C/46° F), inky blackness of a claustrophobic flooded cave passage, the rewards can be great. Rarely, in Wales, does a cave passage continue completely flooded for any great distance; sooner or later the floor rises and a free-flowing, 'dry' passage is regained. Unlike the situation in open water, where diving is undertaken in pairs, the exploration of flooded tunnels is best conducted alone. Yet another contrast with open-water practice is that in a cave the diver must lay out and maintain a firm hold on a guideline, for exhaled air and the movement of the diver's fins disturb the cave-floor sediments. In less than a minute crystal-clear water is transformed to a cloud of mud, the rate of progress is dramatically reduced and the feeling of anxiety begins to mount. To lose the line is to lose all sense of direction!

At Agen Allwedd it was clear that the potential rewards were as great as anywhere in the British Isles. Perhaps the greatest deterrent to exploration was the sheer distance that equipment had to be transported to reach the diving sites. Travelling unencumbered, it could take cavers three hours or so to reach the sumps at either end of the cave; loaded with heavy steel cylinders, pressurised to 200 or more times that of atmospheric pressure—a potentially explosive load—together with other heavy and fragile items of breathing apparatus, the journey could take half as long again.

In 1961 cave divers first entered the flooded pothole in the bed of the river Clydach. Unfortunately, however, the exploration was halted within the space of a few metres as the spring was found to be completely blocked by boulders swept down by the river. It was not until 1966 that the first real success was achieved by cave divers at a site known as Turkey Sump, at the western extremity of Agen Allwedd. The lucky explorers were Mike Wooding and John Sinclair.

In accordance with the normal practice of sump exploration in Britain, only one diver at a time ventures into a constricted underwater tunnel; a second diver waits for a signal—sometimes for several minutes—before following. Within two minutes of Sinclair submerging into the narrow fissure, Wooding received several distinct tugs on the guideline, the prearranged signal that he was through to an airspace. Wooding recounted later:

> I found myself in a wide, dark passage with a jubilant John. We belayed the line and splashed on round the corner to be met, alas, by another sump. I pulled a length of spare line through the first sump and fed it to John as he prospected the new one. He soon returned, having examined the upper 10 ft of a flooded pot in zero visibility. I then dived (base fed by Sinclair) and was able to break through the murk at the bottom of the pot into a clear passage stretching as far as I could see. The passage at a depth of 15 feet was about four feet in diameter, in clean washed, smooth rock with little mud on the floor. I swam rapidly along this section, my hopes rising as the depth fell to 10 feet, then six feet and then five feet. Unfortunately, at this moment the line ran out and I was brought up short. As a last resort, I held the end of the line at full reach, rose to the ceiling and stretched. I was rewarded by the unforgettable sound of a helmet breaking surface and had a tantalising glimpse of a small chamber before being forced to return to base.

A camp scene during the Easter 1959 expedition.

(Photo: *Harold Lord*)

Mike Doggett and Arthur Millett (rear) crossing Turkey Pool. Located some two hours travelling time from the entrance, this obstacle caused the early pioneers some difficulty. In the days before specialised thermal clothing became available, cavers ran the risk of suffering a severe chill or hypothermia after semi or complete immersion in such icy water. To be immobilised after such a wetting is still a daunting experience.

Beyond Turkey Pool lies an extensive series of passages known as Sand Caverns, the floors of which are littered with boulders and loose rock.

Rodney 'Bomber' Beaumont admiring the Swiss Village in the Summertime Series. A conservation tape protects these rare mud deposits, which were formed about 10,000 years ago.

At the head of Turkey Streamway lies Turkey Sump, a point where the walls pinch together and the roof dips beneath the water's surface. Turkey Sump was first negotiated in 1966. Beyond lies well over a mile of 'dry' passage and further sumps.

On a third dive at this site, later in the year, they reached Sump 5. In the process they succeeded in discovering over 600 metres of new, 'dry' passage, by far the most significant discovery for several years. The new section took the cave well beyond the large, dry passages of the Summertime Series, seemingly running parallel to the crags which fringed the western edge of the mountain.

It was not until 1971 that anyone took up the challenge posed by Sump 5. John Parker and Jeff Phillips, of Cwmbrân Caving Club, were perhaps the most accomplished and determined explorers of their day. After two attempts, Sump 5 was passed and a further 600 metres of passages found. Here the cave appeared to come to an end. The pair then set their sights on the other end of the system—the Terminal Downstream Sump—a major project by anyone's standards. With the likelihood of many kilometres of cave still to be found in this particular section, the site was an immensely exciting proposition. The problems, however, were considerable; the distance was greater and the terrain was arguably twice as hard as the route to Turkey Sump. At Easter 1972 a team of valiant 'porters' was recruited to enable Parker to make an epic solo dive into the sump at the end of the cave. Some 278 metres of new passage was discovered, terminating 90 metres into Sump 3.

Deep Water was originally passed with the aid of a dinghy by members of the Chelsea club.

(Photo: *William Maxwell*)

It was July 1972 when Parker and Phillips returned to the Terminal Sump for another assault. Phillips led to the start of Sump 3. Parker then continued alone. In a spacious but meandering passage, route finding proved difficult. Having laid 90 metres of new line, he reached a large underwater gravel bank. His subsequent report read as follows:

> At this point the passage enlarged to 'huge' proportions (50-70 feet wide and 50 feet high). The passage continued like this to a 90 degree corner to the left, where it opened out to about 100 feet wide and 60 to 70 feet high. Several phreatic bridges occurred, some of them spanning 50 feet or more. Main Sump is now 2,000 feet long, average depth 30 feet.

41

It was an incredible dive along a huge tunnel. That day Parker achieved not only a personal record, but also by far the longest dive ever achieved in the British Isles and one of the longest in the world. To venture beyond the point established by Parker was clearly a very daunting proposition.

*   *   *

I had started caving at Llangattock in 1961, at the age of ten; joined Hereford Caving Club soon afterwards and, with youthful enthusiasm, I visited most of the known caves in the area during the subsequent years. My interest soon turned to original exploration. Early in 1967, after considerable prospecting, I discovered Ogof Gynnes, high on Llangynidr moors. This cave, explored in the company of school-mates, was to yield a labyrinth of rifts and muddy tunnels over one kilometre in length. As a 17 year old, the event was to figure as a landmark in my life; from the moment the first turfs were pulled aside to reveal the mysterious opening, I was hooked; the lure of exploration was everything. The course of my life had been determined. I learned to dive at Swansea University, and it was at this time that I teamed up with Roger Solari, an extremely talented caver and cave diver from the Royal Forest of Dean Caving Club. In July 1972 we discovered 1,600 metres (1 mile) of passage in Dan yr Ogof, and in September we made two major breakthroughs in County Fermanagh, Northern Ireland.

Lower Main Streamway in Agen Allwedd.

Roger and I took great interest in the exploits of Parker and Phillips in Agen Allwedd, and in January 1973 we continued from their previous upstream limit, doubling the amount of passage beyond Sump 5 and extending the cave to within a few hundred metres of the Blaen Onneu (quarry) caves, near the highest point on the Llangynidr to Beaufort main road. Early in 1974 we also decided to tackle the Terminal Downstream Sump in Agen Allwedd: this, it seemed, now posed the ultimate challenge in southern Britain.

At this point in time a very

interesting piece of information was brought to our attention. Chelsea Spelaeological Society had produced an extremely accurate (high grade) survey of the main streamway as far as the Terminal Sump. The altitude figures on the plan revealed that there was a difference in height of approximately 46 metres (149 feet) between Sump 1 and the point of resurgence. A basic knowledge of physics indicated that there was no way in which water could 'back up' to such a height. Somewhere ahead lay a major section of free-flowing streamway.

In May 1974 I conducted the first operation alone. That part of the journey beyond the last known airspace, prior to Sump 3, is recorded in my diary:

> The water was brown and murky, the visibility barely one metre. It was simply not possible to gain any impression of the passage size or its characteristics. The only positive guide was the thin orange line disappearing into the blackness. By now my single lamp was waterlogged, shedding a dim pool of light on the sandy floor. I would have felt a little happier had I had some form of reserve lighting, but the cell was reliable and the light output perfectly adequate for the purpose. [Equipment has been greatly improved in more recent years and today, for example, cave divers generally operate with four or more independent sources of lighting.]
>
> Bend after bend passed, and the depth remained roughly constant at about six metres. Eventually I reached Parker's limit, an estimated 230 metres from the start of Sump 3. There was still plenty of line remaining on the abandoned rusting reel, so I quickly belayed mine safely to the outgoing line and moved forward with Parker's.
>
> The depth here was the same, some six metres, and without the guidance of a line I quickly realised that I would have to follow one of the walls. I chose the left-hand wall and, moving cautiously forward, I became altogether more conscious of my air reserves. I had used almost one third of my air supply, the point where the exploration would normally be abandoned—allowing two thirds of the air for the outward journey. [One third of the air is allocated to the outward journey and one third as a safety margin.] It was important not to waste a moment. Suddenly, just 20 metres or so beyond my predecessor's limit, the floor started to rise up a steady incline and, incredulously, 10 metres later my head broke surface. It was almost beyond belief.
>
> Within a few metres I could stand, knee-deep in water. I tied the line to a large stone. This really was incredible. The passage ahead was gloomy and dismal, but equally as large as that prior to Sump 1. Shaking my body violently in order to try and restore the circulation, I moved off into a long, black canal. Then, in the sombre calm of the setting, something else was apparent. There was a quiet, distant rumble somewhere beyond the next corner.
>
> A short swim followed, and 60 metres later a beautiful sight met the eye; the stream flowed away freely over a shallow, gravel bank. With my two cylinders, lead, mask and fins laid carefully to one side, I set off to explore. The passage dimensions soon enlarged to at least 15 metres high by six to eight metres wide. High above, more and more high-level openings were observed, impossible to reach clad only in flimsy wet socks through which every small pebble or sharp rock was apparent. Fortunately, the route proved kind and involved a relatively easy walk.
>
> About twenty minutes down the streamway, I rounded a prominent corner, the roof dipped at a gentle angle and the stream wound its way into Sump 4. The water here

was clear and blue, posing one of the most inviting diving sites that I had ever come across. The kit, regrettably, was nearly 600 metres away. The exploration of this prime site would have to wait.

It was a jubilant, but cautious diver who retraced his steps. Again, everything went smoothly and less than two and a half hours after my departure I was sharing my experiences. The longest sump in the United Kingdom had been passed and a substantial chunk—Maytime—added to the length of the system. Over the length of the new streamway I estimated that there had been a drop of only about six metres. If the new Chelsea survey was correct, it meant that there was a vertical interval of about 39 metres still to be accounted for! Sump 4 was an exciting proposition. If the steady gradient was maintained right through the mountain, as the relatively uniform geology and the findings in the Clydach gorge seemed to suggest, then clearly there was another major section of streamway beyond Sump 4.

The spectacular section of streamway in the Maytime Series, discovered as a result of a diving expedition in May 1974. The two cavers are are the late Rob Palmer and Dave Morris.

Roger and I decided to dive Sump 4 as soon as practical. The date chosen for this operation was 15 June 1974. My diary relates the subsequent events:

The fateful day arrived. It was a glorious summer's morning and, amazingly, many friends turned out to help. It was almost too good to be true. Down through the cave all went smoothly: through the sumps and down the final length of streamway. Despite the weight of cylinders and line reels everything was fine, until we reached that last corner. We reached Sump 4. Previously this had appeared bright and hopeful; today it was peaty and ominous. The place had been completely transformed. There was nothing to raise one's spirits. A distinct feeling of gloom settled upon the scene.

The tragic decision was made. We would dive together, not separately as on all previous explorations. As is normal, we were each responsible for our own decisions and actions, but, as we deposited our boots on a mudbank nearby, we sensed that this sump would not be passed.

Roger led, wearing two medium pressure, 40 cubic foot cylinders. [At shallow depths—for example, six metres—1 cubic foot of air would be expected to last for one minute; 40 cu. ft would be sufficient for 40 minutes.] I followed equipped with two high pressure, 45 cubic foot bottles, and carrying a second 300 metre line reel. From the start Roger was uneasy. He was slightly underweight and shortly began to experience problems with his sinuses. But, despite our mutual concern, he pressed on.

The passage was spacious, the depth gradually increasing: 10 metres . . . 15 metres . . . 18 metres. Eventually, he stopped and indicated 'end of line'. This was at a point 123 metres from dive base. Instinctively, I consulted my pressure gauge. I had already reached my 'one-third margin' on my first bottle; the other was intended for emergency use only, an essential reserve required to exit through Sump 3. The rules dictated that we should now exit. With slightly smaller capacity bottles than mine, Roger's situation was even more pressing.

What happened next was totally irrational. Against all logic and common sense I opted to push on. I presumed that Roger would exit. About 30 metres later I reached a steeply ascending gravel bank. I knew full well that my supply of air was desperately low but I still felt compelled to continue with the reckless gamble. My only thought was that somewhere ahead there just had to be air. From a depth of 22 metres at the elbow of the sump I ascended to a depth of one metre. I reached for the roof but there was no air anywhere! I moved to the right, but it was no use; the roof dipped into an alcove.

At that instant I knew that there was only one remaining course of action. I had to turn back. My pressure gauge now read 50 atmospheres; I had used just over two-thirds of my air. As I turned to exit, there, above me, was Roger. He, too, had been lured inexplicably along this fateful avenue. What utter fools we were. I swam over to him, indicated my intentions, and sped off back down the gravel slope.

Typical cave-diving conditions, near 'black-out'.

That was the last I saw of my friend.

At the bottom, my sinuses were painful owing to my rapid descent and the 'crash' clearance. It was a long way to safety, and any minute I knew that the air in my bottle would run out. I prepared to change mouthpieces. Just over one third of the way back I passed the 'joining of lines' and a little further on I stopped. I prepared for that crucial exchange. With heightened concentration I took a couple of deep breaths, and swapped. The spare breathed easily; one crisis was over.

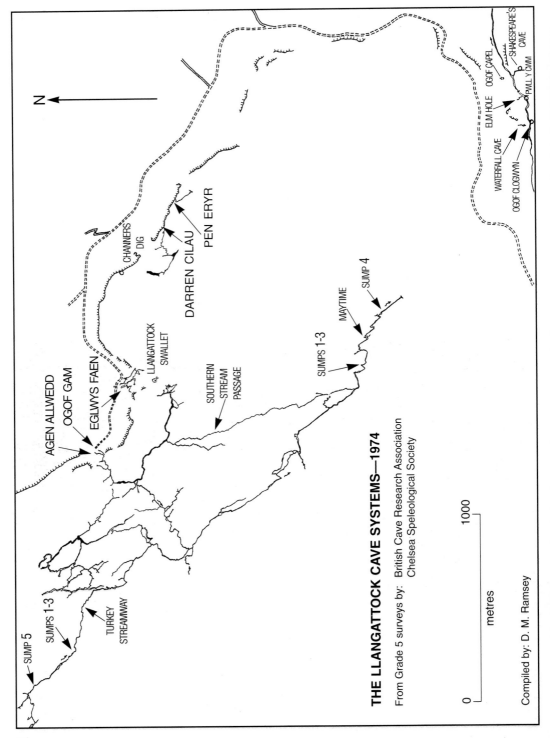

N

SHAKESPEARE'S CAVE

OGOF CAPEL

PWLL Y CWM

ELM HOLE

WATERFALL CAVE

OGOF CLOGWYN

CHANNERS DIG

DARREN CILAU

PEN ERYR

AGEN ALLWEDD

OGOF GAM

EGLWYS FAEN

LLANGATTOCK SWALLET

SOUTHERN STREAM PASSAGE

SUMP 5

SUMPS 1-3

TURKEY STREAMWAY

SUMPS 1-3

MAYTIME

SUMP 4

THE LLANGATTOCK CAVE SYSTEMS—1974

From Grade 5 surveys by: British Cave Research Association
                          Chelsea Speleological Society

0   1000

metres

Compiled by: D. M. Ramsey

I waited for a couple of minutes. Where was Roger? I couldn't feel him on the line. I contemplated going back but realised that I had barely enough air to get myself back to Maytime. By now all the decisions had been made for me.

As my head broke surface, a pain, an excruciating pain, broke out in my head. I stood there in the middle of the pool, agonised, unable to see, think or do anything. The minutes passed, the pain eased, the shock commenced. The dreadful wait began. It was serious. The only hope was that at the furthest point, Roger had located air and was resting before attempting to make his exit. If he allowed the water to clear it was not unreasonable to assume that he might wait several hours.

Two or perhaps three hours later (I had no watch) the terrible discovery was made. By pulling on the line I found that it came in much too freely. I drew it in and discovered that at a point 132 metres from base it had been cleanly cut through. Roger must have become tangled on exit and had to cut himself free. Almost certainly it meant that he had not found an airspace and that in all probability he had lost the outgoing 'safe' line in the process of cutting himself free.

It might all have been a nightmare, a dreadful illusion, were it not for the pair of boots lying on the mudbank. There was nothing more I could do. I collected my remaining gear and walked away in a daze.

I reached Sump 3 and kitted up. There was no feeling of stress, no concern as to the limited air supply in my bottles; just a relaxed, calm resignation. It was all beyond my

Over one kilometre from Sump 4 in Agen Allwedd the cave water finally rises to the surface in the bed of the river Clydach. Pwll y Cwm rising, photographed in the late 1970s, lies in the middle of the river directly in front of the caver.

47

control. I was now in the hands of fate. The two bottles were retrieved at the other side of Sump 3 and soon I was out. Tired and mentally exhausted, I crawled onto the shingle bank. The place was deserted. Everyone had gone.

I reached the entrance to find a distinct light in the sky. Was it dawn? It had to be . . . But, no . . . The final touch to the day's unreal events came in the form of sheet lightning. There was no rain. The night was still and warm. Down in the valley the lights of Crickhowell shone as normal. There were specks of light on the hillside, too; bright, luminous glow-worms by the score. I was desperately confused. How calm and serene everything appeared.

The whole sequence of events still felt like a dream, from which I was only gradually awakening. This was the real world now and the real tragedy would shortly unfold. I reached White Walls and the Cave Rescue Organisation was alerted.

A major rescue was initiated that was to run for the next five days. As with all cave rescues mounted in the British Isles, friends and colleagues came from far and wide to give voluntarily of their time and expertise. No public money or other agency was involved; such is the camaraderie of the activity. Supported by Colin Edmunds, John Parker made two valiant but unsuccessful attempts to recover Roger Solari's body.

A memorial service was held at Holy Trinity Church, Drybrook, on Sunday, 30 June 1974. A short time later a small commemorative plaque was erected near Sump 1.

As the curtain descended upon the tragic finale it appeared that activities in Agen Allwedd had reached a stalemate. The three downstream sumps had yielded to a determined effort but the explorations had proved costly. The cave had claimed its first life. Both downstream and upstream the dry extensions were only accessible to a small number of people. Further progress in these areas was severely restricted. Thereafter the cave settled into a long period of relative inactivity.

Ogof Craig a Ffynnon:
In Search of the Back Door

The sumps at the downstream end of Agen Allwedd formed a very effective barrier to cavers and cave divers alike. All hope of a through trip to the Clydach gorge via this avenue was now ruled out. What other options remained?

Armed with knowledge of the geology, the evident antiquity of the Llangattock caves, and the fact that as the main river cut ever deeper into the limestone it had frequently abandoned one level of cave development in favour of a lower one, the existence of an old 'fossil' route was still a distinct possibility. The huge, ancient Main Passage in Aggy and the complex network of Eglwys Faen gave substance to this idea. Strong draughts in these sections had lured groups to try their luck in awkward sand- and mud-filled tunnels. But the outcome was invariably the same. All too often the digging was difficult or dangerous, and eventually enthusiasm waned.

By comparison, few people had given credence to the possibilities still existing in the Clydach gorge. Caves close to the Pwll y Cwm rising, just above Devil's Bridge, had all proved disappointing. In the absence of a draught, digging was very much a gamble and considered a waste of time.

It was an abandoned quarry site, just above the Rock and Fountain public house, that drew John Parker's attention in 1973. If he wasn't going to get through the mountain by diving, Parker was determined to put another theory to the test. This concerned the behaviour and chemistry of a small resurgence issuing from the base of a steep boulder slope in the

Clydach gorge from Gilwern Hill. The Heads of the Valleys road, the A465, winds its way up the gorge towards Bryn-mawr. The wooded area to the left of the road at the head of the valley is the Cwm Clydach Nature Reserve. The cave streams, which drain from the mountainside to the right, resurge and join the river Clydach approximataly midway along the length of the reserve.

49

The Rock & Fountain Public House (middle distance) from the edge of the beech woods on the south side of the Clydach gorge. The entrance to Ogof Craig a Ffynnon lies in the quarries behind the public house.

John Parker, one of the most determined cave explorers in Britain, and his team devoted much of 1976 to the opening of Ogof Craig a Ffynnon. The exploration of this cave involved tremendous feats of excavation.

Darren Ddu Quarries. Under normal flow conditions this little spring appeared quite insignificant, no different to any of the others in the valley. But after heavy, prolonged rainfall a dramatic flood pulse was common. This suggested something quite unusual, the possibility of some form of overflow cave system, something that might conceivably lead back through the mountain in a westerly direction.

By the summer of 1976 Parker had recruited a small group of friends who made at least two working visits a week to the excavation in the old quarry. One evening Jeff Hill's wife, Jean, discovered a cold breeze issuing from a small hole less than 30 metres from their long-standing dig. At a stroke, their efforts were diverted to the new site and after a few intensive digging sessions they broke into a short section of cave, Ogof Craig a Ffynnon (Rock and Fountain Cave).

At the end of the new cave, water tumbled and a strong flow of air emerged from a distinctly nasty boulder blockage, up through which they slowly began to dig. The normal practice on encountering this sort of obstacle is to remove selectively the smaller stones, leaving the larger ones in place as essential roof supports. Armed with a crow bar, tackling a boulder choke can be compared to a game of chess . . . the skill lying in knowing which block to remove, so as not to bring the roof crashing down! In such a way, the caver moves forward from space to space, though not necessarily in a straight or level course. Occasionally, explosives may be required. Used by licensed holders and in very small quantities (a few grams only), the aim is the same as when using a crow bar or stone chisel—to remove, split or take the corner off a rock to allow one to squeeze past the obstruction.

By November 1976 they had ascended six metres and the choke had been successfully negotiated. The climb was worryingly loose and emerged into a chaotic jumble of boulders set in a slight depression in the floor of a huge chamber. The utmost care was now required to make sure that the route remained open. Craig a Ffynnon had now attained a length of 350 metres, and terminated at the bottom of a sheer, rock-walled climb, an 'aven' in caving parlance. Beyond the 13 metre high rock wall, scaled using rock-climbing techniques, was a far more substantial obstacle, the Second Choke. The draught whistled away, up into another horribly damp blockage. A lot more work lay ahead.

Beyond the First Boulder Choke an awkward 10 metre rope climb gives Huw Durban access to the Second Boulder Choke directly above.

Steve Pedrazzoli emerges from the far side of the muddy confines of the Second Boulder Choke.

Hall of the Mountain Kings, Ogof Craig a Ffynnon.

CAVES OF THE CLYDACH GORGE

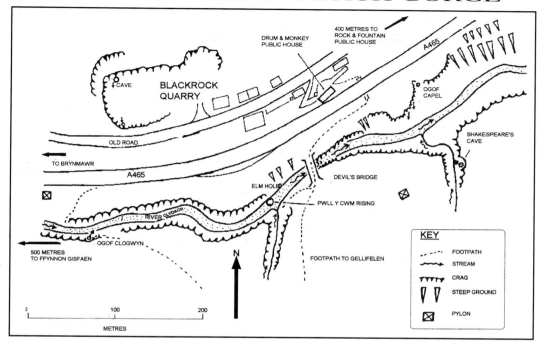

Despite a collapse at the First Choke early in 1977, enthusiasm remained high and after the route was reopened good progress was soon made at the terminal blockage. However, as with all digs, there were times when the group had cause to thank their lucky stars. Russell Pope, after whom the entrance had been named, turned up on one occasion to join the team as they were trying to follow the draught into the first section of the Second Choke. Pope eventually took his turn at the face but all too soon the rate of debris removal slowed to a mere trickle. The other members of the party became impatient; the spoil was not coming out fast enough. But what they didn't realise was that the roof was in an extremely precarious condition and that Pope was keeping a very wary eye on it. Eventually, Hill could stand it no longer:

'Come on, Ben, get out of there. I'll have a go.'

Pope duly retreated and Hill crawled forward. Soon afterwards there was a sudden collapse and Hill's head and shoulders were pinned to the floor. Another regular digging partner, Ann Franklin, quickly pulled one slab away while Parker rushed forward, grabbed Hill's feet and dragged him free. Seconds later, the entire face in front of them collapsed! Hill had been lucky. With just a few facial injuries, he'd got off lightly and, in the time honoured tradition of caving, he later informed his wife that 'he'd fallen out of the entrance'!

As work resumed, a few more people turned up to join the group and help with the digging. For one of them, Bill Gascoine, a local chemistry lecturer, Ogof Craig a

The large trunk passage prior to the major roof collapse at the Fourth Boulder Choke.

The Pagoda formation at the start of the Promised Land.

Close up of the Pagoda.

Ffynnon provided a fascinating new insight into the geology and hydrology of the mountain. Squirming and wriggling up and along the damp, muddy tunnel might not have been the most pleasant way to spend an hour or two but the draught was impossible to ignore.

One evening, an explosive charge was set off that generated an altogether different noise to that of previous detonations. Hitherto the explosions had taken the form of a short, sharp crack; the latest detonation set in motion a loud, dull, echoing rumble. As the fumes dispersed, there was a very real sense of anticipation. Parker pulled back a few rocks and ahead of him he could see a big, black space. A series of shouts confirmed his suspicions. There was a very large cavity just a couple of metres ahead and the draught was howling through the gap. Just one more bang would do the trick. Unfortunately, however, they had run out of explosives!

It was Sunday, 10 July 1977 when the next charge was detonated. In little more than an hour, the fumes had cleared, the rubble was pushed aside and they were through. They had escaped from the miserable confines of the Second Choke. Amid whoops of jubilation, a series of mud-floored chambers interspersed by short crawls, was traversed. They raced on until, suddenly, they reached the top of a boulder pile.

Spread out before them was a breathtaking view; an absolutely enormous tunnel disappeared on into the mountain. At last they had found one of the long sought after 'fossil' passages, trending north-west towards Llangattock. The group quickly scrambled down over the blocks, passed a pool and continued along a fine passage floored with an intricate network of rimstone pools, or 'gours' as they are known to cavers. Each successive pool was impounded by a miniature dam, the overall effect being that of a discoloured, partly frozen waterway, a veritable cascade of flowstone which sparkled like ice crystals in the light of their cap lamps. Such formations were quite unlike anything that they might have predicted. Barely had they come to terms with the beauty of the shallow pools, the reflections and the delicate crystals, when an even larger chamber loomed out of the blackness. Huge stalagmite bosses, akin to mounds of ice beneath a waterfall in deep mid winter, guarded the entrance. Wary of causing any unnecessary damage to the pure white flows, they skirted the chamber, picking their way carefully around its edge.

Only when they had reached the far side of the chamber could they fully appreciate the immensity and true splendour of the scene before them. The chamber was a huge void, 22 metres or more high

Delicate helictites in Helictite Passage beyond the Fourth Choke, Ogof Craig a Ffynnon.

55

and a diameter in excess of its height. Although it was impossible to pick out details of the roof, draped from the upper walls and suspended into the vastness of the chamber was one of the finest flowstone draperies they had ever witnessed. Certainly it was one of the finest sights in British caving. It was a chamber on a par with the largest in Agen Allwedd, and best compared to the huge caverns so often encountered on the continent. For a long while the party stood in awe, slowly absorbing the spectacle. This new wonder was to be named the Hall of the Mountain Kings.

Elation subsequently gave way to disapointment, for ahead lay another huge choke, a blockage extending from floor to ceiling, high above. However, they had added 800 metres (half a mile) to the length of the system which, including all its side passages, was now over two kilometres (nearly one and a half miles). Ogof Craig a Ffynnon now ranked as a classic among British caves.

A ladder climb gives access to further passages and yet more digs high above the Promised Land.

At about this time, Gascoine devoted considerable effort to water-tracing experiments, in an attempt to establish the origin of the little streams seen in the cave. By the following year, 1978, the catchment area had been largely determined. Geologically, there was every indication that the cave would continue its linear trend and lead through the mountain to one or other of the Llangattock caves.

A single digging operation was all that was required to conquer the Third Choke. Another epic advance had been achieved and following additional successful trips, the length of the cave doubled. But the Fourth Choke was to pose a very long and difficult obstacle, not finally overcome until 1979. Beyond lay unimaginable wonders: the largest section of passage in the cave, and a side passage which left the party spellbound. Leading off the north wall, some distance short of the enormous Fifth Choke, lay a passage within which were formations as spectacular as any previously encountered, the perfect complement to the grandeur of the Hall of the

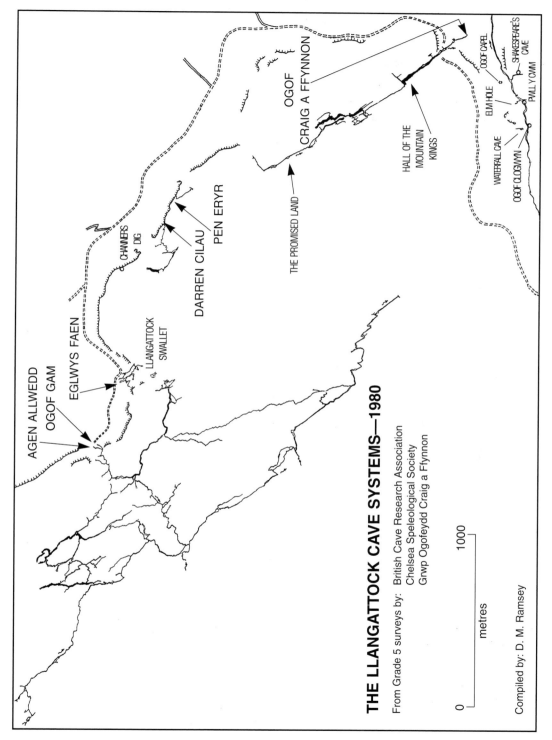

AGEN ALLWEDD

OGOF GAM

EGLWYS FAEN

LLANGATTOCK SWALLET

CHAMBERS DIG

DARREN CILAU

PEN ERYR

THE PROMISED LAND

OGOF CRAIG A FFYNNON

HALL OF THE MOUNTAIN KINGS

OGOF CAPEL

SHAKESPEARE'S CAVE

ELM HOLE

PWLL Y CWM

WATERFALL CAVE

OGOF CLOGWYN

THE LLANGATTOCK CAVE SYSTEMS—1980

From Grade 5 surveys by: British Cave Research Association
Chelsea Speleological Society
Grwp Ogofeydd Craig a Ffynnon

0   1000

metres

Compiled by: D. M. Ramsey

Mountain Kings. One 30 metre stretch of wall was almost completely covered in minute, gravity-defying crystal formations known as helictites. Here, four kilometres from the surface, delicate needle- and bead-like encrustations were to be found in wonderous profusion, an intricate and glorious array unsurpassed in any British cave.

Further exciting discoveries lay beyond a five metre drop in the opposite wall of the main tunnel. Within two weeks, exploration of a one and a half kilometre section, known as the Promised Land, extended the cave far beyond the Fifth Choke, to within 300 metres of Price's Dig, one of the Llangattock caves. Ogof Craig a Ffynnon now measured over eight kilometres (five miles) in length.

Access to this fine system was strictly controlled and many cavers felt frustrated in their failure to book a visit and gain access to the cave. Inevitably, perhaps, the restrictions prompted a reaction, particularly amongst cavers from other areas. Resentment grew and manifested itself in mischief and vandalism. On several occasions the lock on the gate was damaged and on two instances the entire gate was forcibly removed! In April 1979, for example, it was found mounted as a 'prize trophy' on the wall of the Craven Heifer Inn, at Ingleton in North Yorkshire. The police were duly informed but there is little doubt that they regarded the affair with as much amusement as the majority of the caving public. They took no action against the offenders.

Between 1976 and 1979 Ogof Craig a Ffynnon was the scene of a series of spectacular discoveries: today the system is in excess of nine kilometres (nearly six miles). The discoveries also provided a new insight into the geology and hydrology of Llangattock Mountain. Until Ogof Craig a Ffynnon was opened it was generally considered that cave development in the area was restricted to the lower beds of the limestone. With its multitude of pitches and fairly extensive vertical development the Craig a Ffynnon system was found to be significantly different to neighbouring Agen Allwedd. In addition, the new cave boasted a wealth of flowstone formations, features almost entirely lacking in the 33 kilometres of Agen Allwedd. Equally interesting and particularly encouraging was the extent of 'fossil' development. It appeared that the passages had their origin far to the west and north-west, and offered the distinct possibility of a connection with caves at Llangattock.

The hydrological studies undertaken by Gascoine aroused considerable speculation. It had previously been assumed that the subterranean drainage pattern was relatively simple: it was envisaged that one river, namely Agen Allwedd Mainstream, flowed through the mountain, and that all the other streams were tributaries to this flow. The situation at Craig a Ffynnon upset this neat, orderly hypothesis. Furthermore, when fluorescein dye was poured into the small stream at the entrance to Darren Cilau cave at Pant y Rhiw the result was equally fascinating. After a period of 76 hours the dye reappeared in the Pwll y Cwm pool in the bed of the river Clydach. It emerged as a concentrated mass, which appeared to indicate that it had travelled through a separate tunnel to that of the Aggy water. The drainage pattern was evidently far more complex than anyone had contemplated.

The Key to the Mountain: Ogof Darren Cilau

In the early 1980s a new breath of vitality swept Llangattock. Some lengthy digging operations resulted in a series of extensions. At the forefront of the new developments, and arguably the inspiration behind the effort, was Clive Gardener of Chelsea Spelaeological Society. Gardener was to become totally obsessed with the mysteries of Llangattock and it was inevitable that his efforts would lead to a major breakthrough.

In August 1984 Gardener's attention was drawn to Ogof Darren Cilau in the quarries a short distance from White Walls Cottage. Very, very few people ever ventured into this cave, fewer still went twice. A cursory glance at the entrance set the tone of the place. A badger-sized, flat-out watery squeeze led to a low crawl and a set of tight and awkward obstacles, which would occupy the mind and body for at least an hour, or considerably longer, depending on whether or not equipment had to be carried.

About 500 metres from the surface an impressive sight confronted the few who ventured into the cave. Quite suddenly one entered a section of large, old 'fossil'

Clive Gardener of Chelsea Spelaeological Society brought a new breath of vitality to the Llangattock caving scene in the 1980s. His dedication and determination was unparalleled, his enthusiasm infectious.

Although time consuming and sometimes awkward to set up, a radio location exercise such as this allows cavers to communicate with a team on the surface and check upon the accuracy of underground mapping. Left to right: Clive Gardener, Jock Williams, Ian Penny and Dave Mills.

passage, comparable in size to the Main Passage in Aggy. Its exit was blocked by formidable chokes and, frustratingly, there was no obvious place in which to dig. A trip to the end and back could be undertaken in less than four hours, but the unrelenting, gruelling nature of the wet crawls were such that the cave was listed as 'extreme' in the guidebooks.

From the day the cave was first opened, Darren Cilau acquired something of an evil reputation. Those cavers familiar with the site quickly realised that rescue of an injured person from its inner reaches was completely out of the question. The constricted nature of the crawls prevented the use of a stretcher and an immobilised or badly injured caver would almost certainly die. By 1966 some witty member of the Chelsea Spelaeological Society had erected in the caving hut his own little 'reminder' of the consequences of such an accident. Hung conspicuously above the front door was a toy gun. The attached label read, 'Darren Cilau Rescue Kit'—a humorous, yet grisly warning to all intending visitors!

It was a beautiful, warm summer's day when Clive Gardener, Jock Williams and Joe Goodall slid into the constricted watery hollow at the entrance on Sunday, 26 August 1984. As they set out on their journey, a steady draught blew in their faces, the like of which had revealed the initial opening to Vic Howells of the Pontypool-based 'Spinners' group 26 years earlier.

60

Once free of the crawls, they headed directly for the terminal area and started to look around. Just a few metres short of the terminal area there was an obvious depression in the boulder floor, possibly an indication that the underlying sediments had been washed away. Logically, water should flow directly beneath such a depression. However, like most of the large depressions or dolines on the moors above, the slump proved to be a hopeless proposition. There was no way that it could be excavated. Adjacent to the slump, however, Gardener noticed a large boulder that had peeled away from the rock wall, thereby revealing a tight but negotiable crawl. But Gardener's friends were sceptical. To them it appeared as though the fissure, running parallel to the passage, was just an undercut section of the passage wall—a waste of time.

Gardener crawled in, moving the odd rock. Almost immediately he was rewarded by the feel of a draught. A relatively strong flow of air blew out of the hole, similar to that experienced near the entrance. Clearly they had established a very definite new lead.

Just eight metres from the main rift they entered a slight enlargement, a place big enough to turn around. The following Saturday, Gardener and Williams returned and the excavation was resumed. At the furthest, deepest point considerable caution was required as walls, floor and roof were all decidedly loose. Suddenly and quite unexpectedly there was a frightening movement followed by a crashing noise somewhere down below. A stone had evidently fallen free of the choke and clattered down some form of slope. Judging by the booming noise, the cavity below sounded as though it was fairly large.

Mynydd Pen Cyrn and the quarries east of Pant y Rhiw, in which Ogof Darren Cilau is situated. The cave is located in the quarry at the head of the prominent track.

Huw Durban negotiating the dreaded Calcite Squeeze. This point marked the end of the cave until 1963 when a minor enlargement allowed cavers to pass through the squeeze.

Some 60 metres from the entrance, the Vice is an unforgetable obstacle, especially when tired cavers are making their way out of the cave.

Thoughts began to race. Hearts began to thump. They crouched quite still and listened. Beads of perspiration oozed from excited brows and a vision of vast caverns flashed through Gardener's head; exiting, fleeting thoughts troubled by more immediate anxieties. The stability of the entire choke was now in question. Williams was advised to retreat. Hardly daring to breathe, Gardener lay motionless, listening intently for further indications of movement. Minutes passed. There were no more creaks and groans.

What was he going to move next? He looked around again. The left wall, and the roof in particular, was extremely precarious and any attempt to move additional blocks looked likely to disturb the floor, beneath which he knew lay a substantial cavity. Cool nerves and the utmost care was essential.

Time passed. Anxieties began to wane. Williams was recalled and timorously they begun digging again. The most obvious route down was enlarged but whether it was passable was doubtful. Directly above the hole lay a massive boulder slab which, like the proverbial rat trap, appeared to be wedged in place by thin air. It weighed 150 if not 200 kilograms, and in the confines of the constricted space even the slightest movement could prove critical.

When everything possible had been done to secure the boulder, Gardener attempted to squeeze downwards. Feeling around slowly with his feet, he lowered himself cautiously into the hole. Even for a 'ferret' the space was very constricted. Not a word was spoken. Williams could do nothing to help. Waist deep in the squeeze, Gardener was just about to commit himself totally when the unthinkable occurred. Two substantial blocks fell from roof and glanced off his helmet. Gardener was horror-struck, entirely at the mercy of the choke. He braced himself for the inevitable total collapse . . . There was a long pause. The choke was silent.

He had been spared. In those few electrifying moments every ounce of determination had melted away. Ever so slowly, he extricated himself from the hole. It had been a close call. Both Gardener and Williams agreed that they should abandon the place for a week or so; time, hopefully, in which the choke would stabilise.

It was an odd situation. Gardener and Williams were on the verge, or so it seemed, of an exiting breakthrough but lacked the confidence to clear the last offending rocks. Given that the site was hazardous, the normal course of action would have involved the setting of a small explosive charge. In this instance, Gardener deemed the idea too risky as it might initiate a major collapse, thereby ruining any prospects of a breakthrough. Williams summed up their decision:

'We decided to find a caver brave (daft?) enough to do the job for us, and turned to Martyn Farr.'

The following Saturday a group of five entered the cave: Clive, Jock, John Cooper, Paul Tarrant and myself. My diary relates the subsequent events:

Just over 500 metres from the entrance, cavers escape from the confines of the Entrance Passage to reach this substantial section of tunnel. It was not until 1984 that the main access into the cave, situated in the left-wall directly alongside the camera position, was located.

As Clive had related, the site appeared loose and nasty and the roof, above which we had just crawled, was particularly suspect. And, as he'd said, at the terminal point a huge slab was pincered in sideways. In the worse case scenario, it was extremely difficult to predict just what was likely to move first. Stones were dropped through the obvious opening and, sure enough, the echoing rattle sounded fantastic. There might not be a 'pitch' beneath the boulders but there was certainly a very steep slope.

I called for silence and started to enlarge the space. After ten to fifteen minutes, I advised Clive to move back to a safe distance; it was time to remove the final boulder obstructing the hole. I eased down on the crow bar, quite prepared to beat a very hasty retreat. Luck was holding. A moderate force achieved the desired result. The rock came out with little difficulty. This was then quickly manoeuvred to one side and used to prop up the suspect slab in the roof.

The Darren Cilau Rescue Kit! The toy gun hung on the wall in White Walls Cottage, is a grim reminder of the consequences of an accident deep inside this extreme cave.

By now the hole was big enough to enter. I removed my battery pack and, feet first, slowly shuffled my way in backwards. Concern as to the state of the roof was now heightened by an even greater worry about the security of the slab beneath my chest. This was well and truly undermined, and goodness knows what my feet were in contact with. As my backside slid through, I knew that I was committed. For an instant my chest jammed. Experience told me that the gap was about seven and a half inches wide—considerably less than the comfortable 'span of a hand'. Down below, my foot at last found what felt to be a reasonable hold. Concern as to how I was going to reverse this squeeze was forcibly dismissed. There was but one way now: to exhale hard and let gravity do the rest.

The squeeze was painfully tight but in a few seconds I was able to breath a very real sigh of relief. I drew my lamp down behind me and quickly scrutinised my chosen footholds. My head turned and there, directly below, a steep, calcite-coated boulder slope led down into a large passage.

'I'm through . . . there's a big passage . . . Craig a Ffynnon size. Come on down.'

The reflection of Clive's light instantly appeared in the choke above my head. Almost simultaneously Paul relayed the message that at the back, things were not so good. Whilst enlarging the crawl, Jock had badly cut his finger. John, selfless as ever, was going to take him out.

For the moment the ongoing exploration was everything.

'I took my cell off, Clive . . . Suggest you do the same. For God's sake don't touch the roof; keep over to your right.'

Without further ado Clive's boots slid slowly towards me.

Once he was down, I quickly collected a few large rocks and wedged them as best I could beneath our point of exit. Soon, the underside of the choke inspired a little more confidence. Paul then appeared and passed most of the tackle down: a crowbar, ammunition box of food and a large tube of 'emergency gear' (stove, first-aid kit, etc.). Two minutes later a beaming trio were raring to go.

At the foot of the calcite slope an extremely inviting three-metre wide and two-and-a-half-metre high passage disappeared off into the darkness. There was a tremendous sense of occasion. Whooping and laughing we strode off down the passage. Each successive metre seemed to confirm an inner awareness. This advance could well be the one that would, at long last, set us on that long sought after path right through the mountain.

Smooth chocolate-coloured mud and pristine calcite flows led us on. As the passage became bigger, it was abundantly clear that we had achieved an advance on a par with any in the history of cave exploration in the area. There was no restraining our excitement. With 'ammo' box and bar in hand, it seemed to have fallen to me to herald the advance. A metallic drumbeat echoed far and wide, at once destroying the silence of the ages. Three babbling children moved quickly forward.

'The jigsaw is coming together at last, Clive,' I called.

Clive subsequently named the section Jigsaw Passage.

Ten minutes later we entered one of those huge 'fossil' passages so typical of Agen Allwedd, followed by an extremely impressive chamber, today named the Big Chamber Nowhere Near The Entrance. We tottered across an unconsolidated floor of assorted debris and with virtually every footstep blocks slipped or turned beneath our boots. Our spirits were soaring. We raced on. Dripping with perspiration we explored several tunnels trending south and west, a total of about 600 metres of new passage, before returning to the Big Chamber. Turning now in an easterly direction, we scrambled through a low, hands and knees section where, in the dim and distant past, several large slabs of rock had become detatched from the cave roof, obstructing the route with what

Huw Durban in Jigsaw Passage, discovered in September 1984.

we referred to as 'breakdown'. Seconds later another breathtaking sight unveiled itself before our eyes. We were standing at the top of a boulder pile, at the bottom of which another altogether larger tunnel led off into the direction of Ogof Craig a Ffynnon.

Expletives failed us as we strode along this huge, main passage. After ten to fifteen minutes walking, an isolated area of flowstone appeared on the left-hand side; an oasis of white in an otherwise barren world of brown. No words could adequately describe the delicate nature of this incredible array. A flow of pure, glistening, white calcite led up to a fabulous display of helictites draped beneath ledges on the wall. These were by far the finest hitherto encountered under Llangattock Mountain and one of the most beautiful in the country. They were subsequently named the White Company.

The late Ian Rolland studies the Antlers off Epocalypse Passage.

Stewart Baggs admires the White Company, an oasis of white dripstone formations.

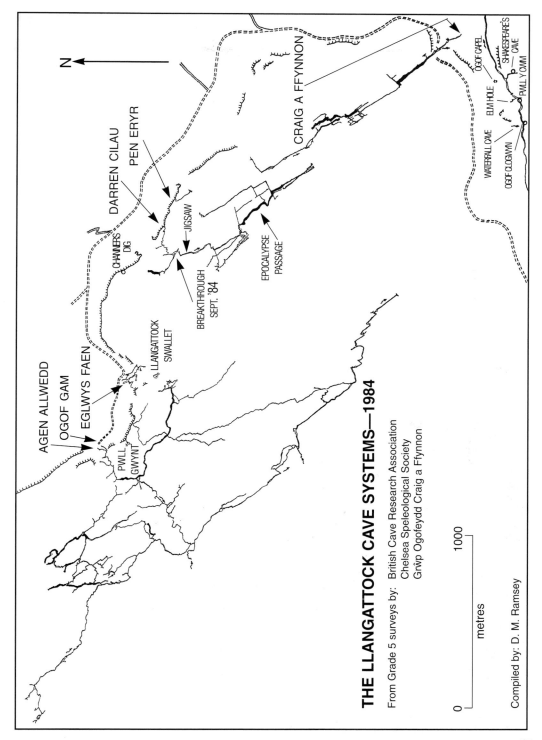

N

CRAIG A FFYNNON

OGOF CAPEL

SHAKESPEARE'S CAVE

ELM HOLE

PWLL Y CWM

WATERFALL CAVE

OGOF CLOGWYN

DARREN CILAU

PEN ERYR

CHAMBERS DIG

JIGSAW

BREAKTHROUGH SEPT. '84

EPOCALYPSE PASSAGE

AGEN ALLWEDD

OGOF GAM

EGLWYS FAEN

PWLL GWYNT

LLANGATTOCK SWALLET

THE LLANGATTOCK CAVE SYSTEMS—1984

From Grade 5 surveys by: British Cave Research Association
Chelsea Speleological Society
Grŵp Ogofeydd Craig a Ffynnon

0   1000

metres

Compiled by: D. M. Ramsey

This was a 'once in a lifetime trip' and we were becoming increasingly awestruck with each successive metre. We marched on. According to the newspaper that morning my star sign, Pisces, shared by Clive, foretold the 'end of an epoch'. After a quiet discussion this superb passage was to earn the name Epocalypse Passage. By now, heads were beginning to reel from all the detail we were trying to absorb, each of us also attempting to establish a mental picture of where we might be under the mountain. We rounded a corner, descended a relatively gentle slope and encountered a small stream. It provided a very welcome drink and another opportunity for a two-minute break. The stream, we thought, had to be that which disappeared in the neighbouring cave, Pen Eryr (a metre high, oval entrance at the south-eastern extremity of Darren Cilau quarry). Leaving the Kitchen we clambered up a steep slope, past a junction on the left-hand side and then gradually began to descend, down-dip, into a crawl. Our luck looked as though it was running out when, to our amazement, we regained height and continued along a large passage once more.

The next feature encountered was a series of funnel-shaped potholes. Somewhere far below us a stream was audible, but without a ladder there was no way down. For some minutes we had been joking about confronting such an obstacle, a pot that would drop us into some taped-off area in Ogof Craig a Ffynnon. Access to this adjoining system was rigorously controlled and we were well aware that any connection made via Darren Cilau would not be viewed favourably. For the moment it seemed that we had the upper hand. I tossed a rock into one of the shafts. There was an almighty crash.

'Sorry, John!' Once more the laughter was uncontrollable.

Walking on past the potholes it looked as though we had a multitude of leads opening up before us. But at this moment the fickle hand of fortune interposed. We reached a major collapse into which, in turn, all the passages seemed to lead. For today, at least, we had met our match. We set off out.

By the time we reached the breakthrough choke we had spent four hours in the new extension, and I had paced out a very conservative 3 kilometres of new passage. Once safely back through the choke, Paul cracked open a celebratory can of lemonade. It had been a remarkable day.

As the year ended, the survey was well advanced. In the space of a couple of months Darren Cilau had been extended from one to five and a half kilometres (over three miles). Sadly, the anticipated connection with Ogof Craig a Ffynnon had failed to materialise. The survey distance between the two caves was probably no more than 150 metres but breaching the final gap was beginning to look like a lost cause.

Clive Gardener, however, was obsessed by Darren Cilau and on an exceptionally bleak St Valentine's Day, 1985, he and Jock Williams made a short but highly significant advance; the addition of a 170-metre extension ending in a series of upward shafts. Soon afterwards, Clive enrolled his team for the big push; climbers to tackle the various high-level leads and surveyors to follow through. By 10.30 a.m. on Saturday, 23 February 1985, thirteen people were *en route* to the St Valentine's Series. By the time they reached the final tall rift, Preliminary Passage, the team members were peering around and babbling excitedly. There were several high-level leads, any one of which might prove successful. Steve Holmes and Adrian Hanson Abbott were to tackle the prime objective, a climb up the terminal boulder blockage, while Tony White, Dick Gledhill and I were to attempt the 'second choice', a short distance short of the choke. Both climbs were sheer and in places overhanging. Neither was an easy option and both required the protection of a rope. Clive quietly stood back and absorbed the spectacle that slowly began to unfold.

We made a six-metre climb to a ledge where Tony geared up in his harness. Never one to waste words, he emptied out his small pack of cave-climbing gear: half a dozen krabs, rather less by way of tapes and a token amount of other hardware. Dick uncoiled the rope. In a matter of minutes Tony was delicately balancing his way across a smooth, rock face virtually devoid of holds.

The 'ledge' was a ledge in name only. It sloped steeply away from the wall before plunging vertically to a floor strewn with massive boulders. As with his surveying technique, Tony was just as cool and meticulous climbing. Every movement was deliberate and calculated; an economy of effort and inspired confidence. With feet clad in wellingtons and a fine film of dark brown mud coating the surface of the rock, Tony certainly did not have the optimum frictional contact that he might have wished for. His harness was tattered and old, well seasoned and well travelled like himself.

After traversing horizontally for six to seven metres, to a point a little over half way to where we hoped there might be a passage opening off the right-hand wall, Tony was faced with a dilemma. There were no eye holes or cracks in which to place protection. Ahead of him the wall was blank. From behind us a tell-tale 'rat-a-tat-tat . . . rat-a-tat-tat' told a similar story. Steve Holmes was having to insert a bolt to aid or protect his ascent. From where Dick and I stood it appeared that this, too, was Tony's only option. He couldn't risk a fall here. One slip and, at the very least,

he would be faced with a long glancing pendulum swing across the rock face, until his fall was arrested beneath his last rope anchor point. An injury here didn't bear thinking about. My thoughts were drawn again to the toy gun, the 'Darren Cilau Rescue Kit' hanging above the door in White Walls Cottage. There was no need to say anything. Like the computers he operated in every-day life, Tony was only too well aware of the consequences of his actions.

'How are you doing?' enquired Dick.

The Pin Cushion: clusters of spectacular calcite formations in Urchin Oxbow, a side passage leading off Epocalypse and linking with Antler Passage.

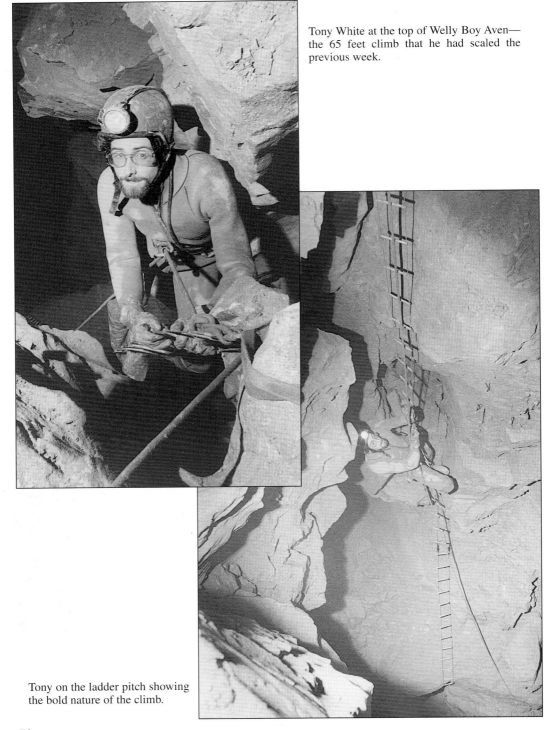

Tony White at the top of Welly Boy Aven—the 65 feet climb that he had scaled the previous week.

Tony on the ladder pitch showing the bold nature of the climb.

'I'm going to try and lasso the large boulder in front of me.'

About five metres in front of him stood a monumental boulder set into the mouth of the presumed passage. Without a doubt it weighed several tons but its stability was very much in question. Much larger boulders than this had been known to peel off rock walls. Tony clearly thought it worth the risk. Down below the observers were instructed to stand well clear.

Tony made himself as secure as possible and then drew in all the spare rope. From the limited amount left over he fashioned his lasso. The technique might have been somewhat unorthodox but, amazingly, in minutes a coil lay around the rock. Then, ever so gently, he eased himself over. It was all very impressive.

'There's no passage,' shouted Tony, 'it's just an alcove . . . but there looks as though there might be something at the head of the next climb.'

Our end of the rope was left attached as a fixed traverse line and, by the time Dick and I crossed the ledge, Tony had reorganised himself ready to tackle the next section. There was now much less rope available to tackle the next vertical climb. Although no more than 13 metres in height, the top was at least 20 metres above the floor, and the exposure factor was considerable.

With few words Tony set off. I found the lack of communication frustrating. Dick and I were keen to know what he was up against; keen to know what he could see above. But we had to do without the spoken word; evidently Tony was giving the climb his utmost concentration. The odd rock crashed into the depths. Somewhere down below Clive would be listening equally intently; after all it was his efforts that were directly responsible for this particular advance and he, no doubt, would be as anxious as we were.

For a progress report we looked to the rope. We knew that Tony was almost there. Then, suddenly, about half an hour after he'd left us, a long awaited call echoed down.

'I'm at the top . . . and there's a fair sized passage heading off in both directions.'

The tone of Tony's voice was distinctly enthusiastic. The lead was obviously extremely interesting. There followed another pause. Tony would now be securing the rope. At long last that all important instruction reached our ears:

'Come on up.'

In turn, Dick and I krabbed onto the fixed rope and free climbed up to join Tony. Now we could see for ourselves just what he had been up against. The climb was exceptionally bold, with a slightly overhanging chimney-like scoop occupying the last four to five metres. Our congratulations were met with a broad grin. Tony was justifiably well pleased with himself. Welly Boy Aven had been scaled and, at a first glance, the prospects appeared excellent.

Moving off in an easterly direction, 90 metres of easy passage led to a deep shaft, even deeper than the aven up which we'd just climbed. Darren Cilau was rapidly developing into something of an obstacle course. Where we stood, the shaft was about two to three metres in diameter but, below, it belled out into a much, much bigger void. The most exciting discovery, however, was the sound of running water which could plainly be heard down below us; a stream that was evidently much larger than anything previously encountered in the cave.

There was no way of descending the shaft without tackle—equipment we did not have at our disposal. But fortune smiled upon us. On our return to Welly Boy Aven, Steve and Adrian had concluded their activities. They had descended from their route and were in the process of packing their gear away. After explaining the situation, Dick climbed back down, and soon we were in possession of an extra rope and two seven-metre lengths of ladder.

The new shaft was rigged but it soon became clear that the ladders would not be long enough to reach the floor. Might it be possible to climb down the bottom section of cave wall? Tony went down to take a look.

'I'm at the end of the ladder,' he shouted. 'I can see the floor about nine metres below me; it's free-hanging all the way.'

The thin wire ladder was evidently suspended in space, well away from either wall. That's the end of our activities for the day, I thought.

All went silent again. The minutes passed. What was Tony up to? Unbeknown to us, he had found further inspiration. Like a spider suspended in space, industriously endeavouring to construct a new web, Tony assessed the options in his precise, clinical manner. He quickly devised another unorthodox technique. Still attached to his harness was his climbing hammer and a few tapes. After tying a length of tape to the hammer, he decided to try and lodge the latter in a small alcove very close to where he was now hanging. If successful, he would then pull himself into the wall, re-belay the ladders and make his way to the bottom for a brief look around.

After a couple of throws the hammer was in place. He eased himself across, 'landed', and made himself secure. His short instruction informed us of his actions and intentions:

'I'm off ladder, in a very small alcove. Lower the ladders down. I'll re-belay them here and then you can line me to the bottom.'

With a distant but distinct tinkle, the ladders were carefully lowered into the darkness. A few minutes later Tony was ready to resume his descent. The rope was fed quietly into the shaft. Tony was about to establish precisely what lay ahead. Seconds later he reached the floor. He unclipped the rope and once more all went quiet. The minutes seemed like an eternity. At long last muffled footsteps and a flickering reflection returned once more.

'Take in. Climbing.'

Slowly the same routine was followed in reverse. The suspense was unbearable. Tony's beaming face suddenly came into view, and his look said it all. Tony, normally cool and emotionless, was very excited.

At the bottom of the shaft there was a huge sand- and boulder-floored passage. Meandering through the debris was a small stream which he had followed as far as a massive rockfall located 70 metres upstream. Downstream, however, he had followed the passage for over 200 metres. At the furthest point downstream, Tony encountered the top of a steep boulder pile, beneath which the stream flowed into a tall, wide rift.

Having convinced himself that the rift continued in a downstream direction, he came to the decision that if this was the long sought after key to the mountain, then the exploration should be shared by all those whose efforts had led to this major advance.

All the tackle was left in the cave, and 9 hours after entry the day's findings were being discussed at the cottage. An examination of the survey confirmed our hopes. A bearing of 154° (south-east) had been taken looking down the new streamway, precisely the orientation we had hoped for. The new extension ran parallel to Epocalypse and headed in the direction of the massive blank area between Ogof Darren Cilau and Ogof Agen Allwedd, to the west.

Considering the number of cavers who received word of this exciting new development, it was astonishing to find that only seven turned up to join the exploration the following weekend. Apart from Tony, Dick and myself, the party

The 70-foot ladder pitch leading down into White Passage, on the day of the big discoveries.

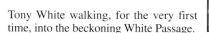

Tony White walking, for the very first time, into the beckoning White Passage.

included Clive, Arthur Millett, Dave Mills and Gavin Crook: seven extremely excited cavers who, from the outset, viewed the prospect as the most significant development since the original breakthrough the previous September. Clive and I took charge of the photographic gear, while the rest carried food and a vast amount of tackle.

It had been agreed that this exploration would be conducted as a team. This meant that there was quite a delay before the last man, Arthur, was safely down the 22-metre pitch. By now everyone was champing at the bit. As we moved off over the boulders into White Passage (named by Clive in recognition of Tony's contribution to the exploration of the system), the excitement was electrifying.

We reached Tony's previous limit, clambered down and tramped on. About five minutes later we reached the foot of a steep but short bouldery slope leading upwards into blackness. Debris slipped and rolled beneath our feet as we carefully scrambled to the top. We emerged onto a platform or balcony of huge rock slabs, lightly peppered with delicate hair-like selenite crystals. We had entered an enormous chamber, one of the largest in the British Isles and, in a minute or so, a full complement of lighting had been assembled which allowed us to survey the awe-inspiring scene set out before us. Ahead lay not just a large chamber but rather an immense trunk passage, one of the ancient arteries of the mountain.

Feeling humbled we moved off into the huge passage that Tony later named the Time Machine. Who on earth could ever have foreseen that such a cavern lay beneath this mountain? In places, the passage was so tall that the roof was well beyond the range of our lamps—an estimated height of well over 25 metres. Boulders the size of small buildings lay scattered about haphazardly; huge, tottering piles of slabs that demanded the utmost respect: up, down, over and around; a never ending obstacle course. We had embarked on a flight of pure fantasy.

After about 500 metres the huge passage terminated abruptly at a boulder fall, a blockage that, at first glance, appeared to fill the passage from floor to ceiling. Just a few metres short of the choke, however, at the bottom of a 10-metre descent, there seemed to be a way ahead at stream level. Nine times out of ten a massive roof collapse, such as the blockage encountered, would have filled the passage. Like a massive avalanche or landslide, the boulders would have 'flowed' into every recess, hopelessly blocking the way forward.

Prepared for the worse, we scrambled down an easy slope only to discover that we could walk around the side of the choke! We were on our way again. Within a few metres there was an abrupt turn to the right and it became immediately apparent that we had parted company with the old 'fossil' passage. We were now in a smaller streamway, a smaller version of Turkey Streamway in Agen Allwedd. Our luck was holding. Arthur confirmed that we were on a bearing of 150 to 160 degrees and were heading 'down dip', down the gently sloping rock strata, into the very heart of the mountain. Spirits soared once more.

We reached a prominent junction where another sizeable stream entered from the left.

'I bet that's from the end of Epocalypse,' said Clive.

Judging from the distance and direction that we had travelled, Epocalypse certainly seemed the most likely source. We had regained the stream which flowed from Pen Eryr to Antler Passage, and which ultimately disappeared beneath the blockage at the end of Epocalypse. This meant that we were now well into the uncharted territory which separated Agen Allwedd from Craig a Ffynnon.

We raced on. Within 100 metres we climbed up a short boulder slope. Here, about eight metres above our heads, a huge 'fossil' passage crossed our path, the aptly named Flyover.

'That's the way to Craig a Ffynnon,' said Clive.

The tunnel, at least six metres in diameter, headed off due east, directly towards Ogof Craig a Ffynnon. After a momentary pause, it was down the other side of the boulder slope and onwards in a downstream direction.

Our mentor, Clive, appeared to have visualised the entire complex of passages beneath the mountain. Quite apart from the sheer dogged tenacity that he had displayed in the search for this new lead, he had perused the ever growing survey for hours on end in an attempt to establish patterns and trends from the mass of irregular, twisting and turning lines. He had devoted himself tirelessly to this quest and each of us felt a sense of gratitude in his presence.

By now there was a very real sense of anticipation. At long last it felt as though we had the key to the entire mountain in our grasp.

'I've dug 20 years in and around the mountain for this,' said Arthur.

Tony and I, both members of the South Wales Caving Club, began to reminisce about our early days. We'd both been caving since the early 1960s but, unfortunately, had missed out on the major discoveries in the Swansea valley. In 1966 and 1967 Tony, then a student at Leeds University, was actively involved in the exploration of Pennine caves, whilst I was still at school and exploring locally.

For us all, this was now a classic trip, destined to become an indelible memory; a once in a lifetime discovery.

'Twice in a lifetime!' retorted Clive, as he recalled that incredible day the previous September. How distant that now seemed, yet in the annals of cave exploration at Llangattock it was a date to remember.

The pace did not ease for an instant. Rocks tottered and turned as we slid and stumbled on greasy, cave-floor deposits; it was a frantic, headlong dash ever deeper into the mountain. There were formations dotted here and there, better than those in the Main Streamway of Agen Allwedd, but none comparable to the White Company or the Antlers. Perhaps the most notable was the small helictite growth which our biologist, Dave Mills, dubbed the Bonsai. This beautiful little formation resembled a miniature oriental tree, with the added curiosity of a small 'rabbit' crouched on one of its branches.

The gradient and bearing, confirmed by Arthur's frequent checks, continued much the same. Surely nothing could stop us now, other than the terminal sump, the base level for the system. Perhaps we might even reach the main streamway, that final stretch of free-flowing water that must surely exist beyond Sump 4 in Agen Allwedd. Hopes were high; the passage wide open.

Eventually, the stream disappeared into a tight fissure leaving us to continue along the spacious, mud- and sand-floored King's Road. Gradually, it was becoming clear that the passage was getting smaller. The floor, walls and roof were plastered in thick deposits of mud. We were approaching the water-table. Stooping ever lower, we suddenly heard the murmur of a stream. Around a corner the floor dropped away and we were confronted by a prominent T-junction. Ahead of us lay a spacious passage occupied by a small stream.

The significance of this discovery was not lost; one route provided us with a passage towards the Clydach gorge, towards that elusive Agen Allwedd streamway, while the other, equally as important, was an obvious avenue leading in a westerly direction. There was a sombre feel to the place. The small stream flowed along a muddy, flat-roofed passage about three metres high and six metres wide. The clean, washed floor, however, gave a clear indication that a major stream flowed here in times of flood. It appeared to be some form of overflow passage.

Tony suggested that it was time for a break, a bite to eat and a chance to cool down. His glasses were well steamed up and giving him trouble; they required cleaning. As we sat down and took some well earned nourishment, it suddenly dawned on us that we were now six hours in from the entrance, and much of that time had been spent on the move.

At the T-junction, just short of the Darren Terminal Sump. From left to right: Clive Gardener, Richard Gledhill, Arthur Millett, Dave Mills, Gavin Crook and Tony White.

Beyond the Pitches and some two and a quarter hours travelling time from the entrance, is the largest underground passage in Britain—the Time Machine: the passage here is about 30 metres wide and 25 metres high.

(Photo: *Gavin Newman*)

The Terminal Sump in Darren Cilau. Muddy and oppressive, it takes over three hours travelling to reach this point, which lies about 550 metres from the Pwll y Cwm rising, in the bed of the river Clydach.

Less than ten minutes later we moved off down the passage. Barely had we got into our stride, than a large stream was found welling up from beneath the right-hand wall. The water was coloured bright green. Instantly, there was an almighty cheer. Our spirits had been revitalised and we were as excited as we had been some two hours earlier when we entered the Time Machine. The stream owed its colour to fluorescein. Bill Gascoine had poured 200g of the dye into the disappearing surface stream at Llangattock Swallet (above and very close to Eglwys Faen cave) the day before—a carefully coordinated trace planned to coincide with our exploration of the innermost reaches of the cave. This was the first time that this water had been identified underground and it meant that we now had a positive lead taking us back in the direction of Eglwys Faen, some two miles distant. For the moment, however, this was an upwelling—a sump—and there was no way forward.

We turned away and continued our downstream journey. The ongoing passage was now a dark canal, gradually deepening and occupying more of the floorspace. Tony's call came as no shock:

'Looks like a sump.'

He edged forward along the left-hand wall and, sure enough, the roof gradually dipped before finally intersecting the water's surface. This was journey's end. The ongoing sump was big and open, a relatively easy dive. But such thoughts were quickly dismissed. We still had a major dry lead to explore, namely that upstream of the T-junction.

As we headed upstream it was apparent that all of us were beginning to tire. Psychologically, we had hit a low point. We were at least five hours caving time from the entrance—a journey involving an unrelenting succession of obstacles, demanding the utmost concentration. One slip might spell disaster. Rescue was impossible. Fatigue served to highlight the dangers. Spirits were inevitably subdued and the prospect of embarking on further exploration was daunting. How far might the passage go? In a straight line all the way to Llangattock Swallet, over three kilometres away?

For the moment, all members of the team were in agreement and we were all for pushing on up the dark, watery tunnel. We hadn't been going for more than three or four minutes when we skirted a large mound of debris. Beyond lay an ominously deep pool. Was this a lake or a sump?

Not all of us were equipped with wet suits, so while the main body of the group waited for the verdict, Tony and Arthur took the initiative. They waded into the murky brown water and within a few metres commenced swimming, disappearing around a corner to the left. The rest of us were under no illusion; ahead lay a long, cold immersion! Seconds later Arthur's voice sounded loud and clear:

'It's a 16 metre swim . . . just goes on like before.'

This was the moment of decision. Dick was wearing dry gear, and Clive didn't like deep water. The two, therefore, would slowly make their way back up Bonsai Streamway, exploring the various side leads. Gavin also decided to join them. I swam over to join Tony, Arthur and Dave.

Tony led on. After rounding a couple of corners we were confronted by a bright green lake. We had rejoined the Llangattock Swallet streamway. But here our hopes were dashed. A few metres ahead water emerged from a shallow looking sump. Other than by diving, there was no way on.

A pace and compass survey and further exploration was undertaken as we made our way to the surface. We raced around, dripping with perspiration, as we attempted to tie up loose ends. By now our work was developing into a race against time but our bodies were revitalised as each fresh lead opened up before us. By the time we had pushed into the choke at the end of Half Mile Passage it was time to admit that we had not only pushed our bodies but also our luck. How much more could we expect from our lights? I had a lead-acid lamp reliable for a period of 10 hours or so on the powerful main beam, perhaps 13 if I was careful. We had now been underground for 12 hours!

Psychologically, once the pitches were behind us we were 'out'. The route ahead was relatively straightforward, though a very long haul. Picking our way by the meagre illumination of the small pilot light demanded concentration. Conversation ceased. It would take over two hours to reach the entrance. We were all tired but Gavin was exhausted.

From left to right: Clive Gardener, Tim Allen, Peter Bolt, Henry Bennett and Mark 'Gonzo' Lumley surface after a nine-day camp based at the bottom of Darren Cilau. Exploratory missions lasting several days or more were common after 1985. The last three cavers are members of the Rock Steady Crew who conducted many successful explorations in Darren Cilau in the late 1980s.

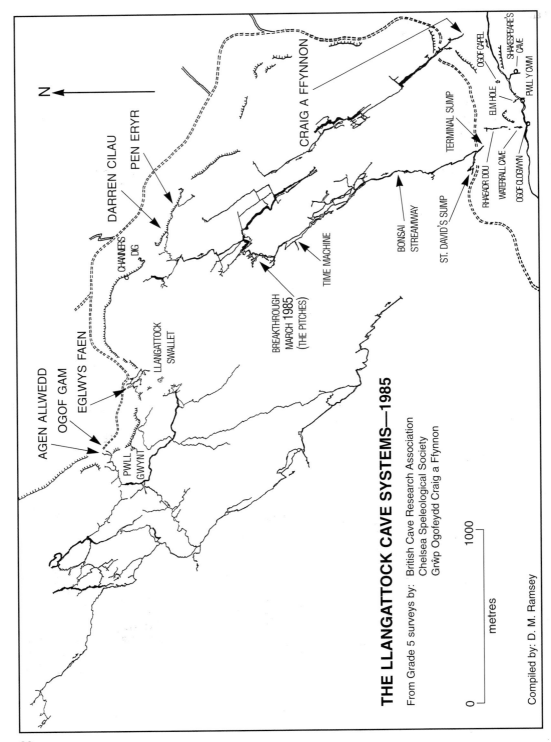

THE LLANGATTOCK CAVE SYSTEMS—1985

From Grade 5 surveys by: British Cave Research Association
Chelsea Speleological Society
Grŵp Ogofeydd Craig a Ffynnon

Compiled by: D. M. Ramsey

N

AGEN ALLWEDD
OGOF GAM
EGLWYS FAEN

PWLL GWYNT

LLANGATTOCK SWALLET

CHANNERS DIG

DARREN CILAU
PEN ERYR

CRAIG A FFYNNON

BREAKTHROUGH MARCH 1985 (THE PITCHES)

TIME MACHINE

BONSAI STREAMWAY

ST. DAVID'S SUMP

TERMINAL SUMP

RHEADUR DDU
WATERFALL CAVE
OGOF CLOGWYN

ELM HOLE

OGOF CAPEL

SHAKESPEARE'S CAVE

PWLL Y CWM

0   1000

metres

'This is the longest trip I've ever been on,' he confided. 'Never done more than 10 hours before.'

Back in Jigsaw, Gavin was reduced to snail's pace. He was on his last reserves.

'I'm having a 10 minute rest, then a 5 minute stop.'

Gavin was absolutely knackered. We agreed to a two-minute stop before moving on.

Everyone kept going and that was all that really mattered. As the first four emerged from the entrance only one light was still working! The rest were down to their final glimmer. We had been underground for 16 hours and we'd explored about five kilometres (three miles) of new cave.

Back in the cottage seven weary bodies shed their caving gear. After what was possibly the most successful day in the history of British caving there were smiles all round. Clive produced a survey and dirty fingers stabbed at the relevant sector. We had completely by-passed Ogof Craig a Ffynnon and had breached the crucial area adjacent to Ogof Agen Allwedd. There were new leads all over the place. Clive's eyes brightened; that obsessive look once more crept across his face. He began to hypothesise:

'The volume of water in Llangattock Swallet streamway is far more than that from Darren Cilau . . . there's one more "once in a lifetime trip" to come!'

The connections looked imminent. If the three major systems were joined the complex, as a whole, would be the longest in the British Isles. We were on the verge of re-establishing Llangattock as the location of Britain's largest cave system, a position Agen Allwedd had gained in 1959 and then relinquished in the mid 1960s. Yesterday's fantasy was on the verge of becoming tomorrow's reality.

The First Connection

Ogof Darren Cilau was now well and truly in the national caving limelight. Since September 1984 the cave had been extended from one to over twelve kilometres, and situated as it was midway between Agen Allwedd and Craig a Ffynnon, few could now doubt that it was very much the key to the mountain.

Such was the pace of activity that within two weeks of the second major breakthrough nearly all the open leads had been explored, and, once more, cavers were resigned to digging. Strategically, the sumps were well placed: that at the downstream terminus lay 500 metres from the resurgence, while the upstream St David's Sump lay approximately one kilometre from the downstream Sump 4 in Agen Allwedd. But there was no easy way of tackling the sumps in Darren Cilau. Diving into the cave from the rising above Devil's Bridge in the Clydach gorge had to be ruled out: it was completely blocked. The only other possibility was the sump in Elm Hole, which was believed to connect with the underlying main drainage network. But, given the highly constricted nature of this site, both above and below water, no one had attempted to penetrate the route since my exploration in 1974.

A month after the discovery of the Darren sumps the arduous bottle-carrying sessions began: for example, it took seven hours to transport the first bottles to the bottom of the cave. On 27 April 1985 the late Ian Rolland* and I made the first exploration at St David's Sump, the streamway which promised to lead back towards Llangattock. An easy 55 metre dive yielded a kilometre of spectacular tunnel leading to a large chamber, the walls and roof of which were plastered in thick mud deposits. Its floor angled away steeply down into the Gloom Room, one of the most ominous looking sump pools I had ever seen. In theory, the distance to Agen Allwedd had now been halved; the remaining distance from the Gloom Room being of the order of 500 metres.

The explorations beyond St David's Sump were lengthy and tiring. By contrast, the trip to the terminal downstream sump was short and required only the normal portering support. A carrying party could reach the sump in less than five hours which rendered this objective an ideal fall-back, if time was short or one wasn't feeling up to scratch.

Concurrent with the commencement of diving activity at the end of Darren Cilau, John Cooper now activated a long-standing project not too far distant—that of digging out the Main Rising, Pwll y Cwm, in the Clydach gorge. The idea of a dig here had been first mentioned as early as 1982 but the dramatic discoveries in Darren Cilau

---

*Ian Rolland died on 27 March 1994 on a cave-diving expedition to Mexico. At the time he was actively exploring an underwater tunnel in the Huautla cave system, one of the world's deepest and most challenging caves. His body was located by his diving partner, Kenny Broad, further into the cave than anyone had been before, 'resting peacefully on the edge of beyond'.

At the end of Psychotronic Strangeways (beyond St David's Sump) Ian Rolland peers into the murky depth of the Gloom Room Sump. This obstacle was finally passed in 1995 by Rick Stanton diving from the newly opened Pwll y Cwm entrance. A further kilometre of passage lies beyond, taking the cave to within a few metres of Sump 4 in Ogof Agen Allwedd.

Martyn Farr, fully kitted and about to dive into the very unpleasant tunnel of Elm Hole, close to Pwll y Cwm rising.

(Photo: *Stewart Baggs*)

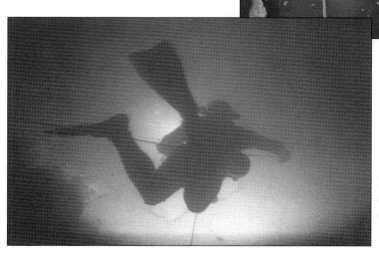

Atrocious visibility is typical in the terminal sump of Darren Ciliau. Such conditions render exploration slow and difficult.

prompted the formulation of a realistic plan and a determined assault. The advantage of having an 'easy', direct back-door to the mountain was obvious. Masterminded by John and supported by a host of others, work commenced in the early summer 1985.

A barrier to prevent further debris from being washed into the hole was an essential first step. In essence, this was achieved by diverting the stream in order to concentrate its flow along the south bank. An airlift was devised and this soon proved a major asset in the removal of very fine silt. A large A-frame scaffold facilitated the removal of larger rocks. All those familiar with the Clydach gorge, and the work entailed, realised that it might take several years before success was achieved. For the time being, therefore, it was not possible to pin any hopes of easy access to Darren Cilau via the Clydach gorge route.

My first dive downstream in Darren Cilau took place in May 1985; it was the start of the underwater link-up operation. The most memorable aspect of the first exploration of this section was not the length of line laid (eventually 140 metres) but rather a heart-stopping encounter about 20-25 metres into the dive. Just as I was getting the feel of the sump—a large flat-roofed passage festooned with boulders and fine silt—an alien object appeared through the murk. The visibility, quite typically, was atrocious—about 1.5 metres—but there before me stood what any mortal would have identified as a ghost; a white-shrouded apparition.

It was a moment of pure horror, a totally unexpected, real-life spine-chilling experience. Terror commandeered my body. Who, or what, was this thing that stood in silent vigil in my path? And worse still, it was as though I was caught in some bewitching spell, under the influence of which I was powerless. My forward motion through the murky water made it impossible to turn and flee; I was drawn inexorably forward. As wild thoughts flashed through my head, reality, mercifully, dawned. I had come face-to-face with, of all things, Bill Gascoine's big lycopodium net,* which had been washed away in a previous flood!

Psychotronic Strangeways: a spectacular tunnel discovered by diving St David's Sump in April 1985.

*A lycopodium net is a very fine-meshed net used to catch the minute spores of the lycopodium fern, which may be dyed different colours. Introducing different coloured spores into different streams gives a lot more information concerning water origin than fluorescein dye.

During the third operation at this site, in March 1986, the line was extended yet further, from 230 metres to 330 metres from dive base. Despite the poor visibility, the depth remained relatively shallow, less than 10 metres. However, 310 metres into the flooded passage there was a sudden 'drop-off', a wall-like feature beneath and beyond which the floor continued altogether deeper (15 metres) and the passage more substantial. This was a significant development. On the basis of previous dives at Elm Hole in 1974 I had come to the conclusion that the underwater route from Agen Allwedd, Darren Cilau, etc. to the resurgence was deep. At 310 metres downstream in Darren Cilau, the depth and larger passage dimensions seemed to confirm earlier findings, and also suggested that the connection was not far from being achieved.

However, if a connection was to be made between Darren Cilau and the Clydach gorge it was felt all along that the final work would have to be accomplished at the Elm Hole end. It was wholly impractical carrying more and more bottles into Darren Cilau. The focus of attention thus changed to the Clydach gorge.

Despite initial optimism, it was now clear that the Pwll y Cwm project was destined to become a long-term affair. The 'easy' access route was ruled out. If a dive connection was to be achieved, it would have to be via that tortuous length of passage nearby, Elm Hole. I had made two exploratory dives in Elm Hole in 1974 before the site had been deemed too hazardous to pursue. No one had been back since.

Having more than halved the distance from Darren Cilau to the Clydach gorge on 22 March 1986, I ventured to Elm Hole nine days later. If this flooded tunnel led to Darren, then surely the remaining gap of 200 metres or so could be closed in the space of a couple of dives? With vastly improved equipment, new techniques and a wealth of experience acquired since 1974, the psychological barriers were brushed aside.

But the dream was dashed. On diving Elm Hole the place was found to be exceedingly intimidating; in visibility of barely one metre I wriggled and bumped forward a mere 30 metres, nowhere near as far as the point reached years earlier.

Twelve days later I was psychologically reattuned. The main tunnel was regained after a lapse of twelve years. I knew that Darren Cilau lay in a north-westerly direction but, as I moved off along the right-hand wall, the passage headed south-westwards! But 25 metres further on, virtually beneath the surface river bed, a sharp corner was rounded, the depth reached 22 metres and, at long last, the passage headed off in the required direction. I knew that my air supply would not last long at such a depth, and each time I checked the contents gauge there was a very real twinge of anxiety. Every breath was precious but no amount of self control could prevent that delicately balanced needle falling back visibly in front of my eyes. I emerged, as on previous dives, feeling absolutely drained. Elm Hole was far from straightforward. The line reel had been dropped just 30 metres from a point known as the Corner, 200 metres short of the end of the Darren Cilau line.

Owing to the constricted nature of Elm Hole the use of large diving bottles was

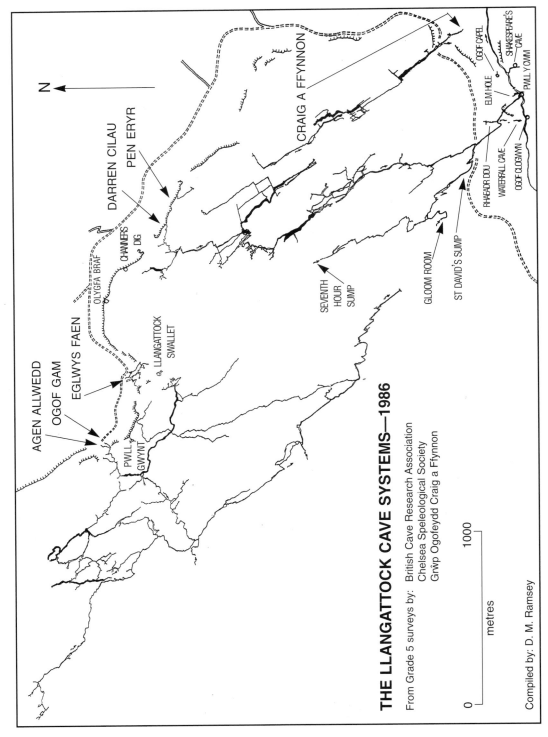

THE LLANGATTOCK CAVE SYSTEMS—1986

From Grade 5 surveys by: British Cave Research Association
Chelsea Speleological Society
Grŵp Ogofeydd Craig a Ffynnon

Compiled by: D. M. Ramsey

out of the question but on 4 May I advanced another 40 metres, 70 metres in total from the Corner. On 22 June, the standard British arrangement of using two bottles was supplemented by the addition of a third, hand-held 'stage' bottle. It was a real struggle passing the constricted Elm Hole rift but the additional supply allowed me to reach a point 250 metres from the diving base. Here, the depth eased to 20 metres and according to my survey there could only be a very short distance to go. Even so, the next dive required four bottles. Because it was physically impossible trying to wear or, indeed, carry four bottles through the rift, a 'staging' dive was undertaken on 29 June in order to deposit another line reel and a full bottle at the Corner for the next push.

I had almost reached my psychological limit. On 3 July there was a very real air of tension. Barely had I submerged than complications arose: the air in the hand-held bottle was difficult to breathe, and my mask was leaking slightly. As I slid down the rift, my face pressed tightly against the rock, I jammed. After a momentary delay I was free but deep inside my head my own delicate control mechanism had been unsettled. I moved on. 'Try to relax; keep calm,' I told myself. But as each exhalation exploded into the confines of the dreadful passage, I was acutely aware that the time clock was ticking away.

By the time I reached the Corner and the full bottle deposited there four days previously, I realised that not only was I a little heavy but that I would also have to watch out for loose line on exit. As ever, there was no time to look around, no time to waste. I was an intruder in an alien environment and I had no intentions of spending a minute more than was absolutely necessary.

I ripped off the protective polythene bag over the mouthpiece of the 'staged' bottle and started on the second cylinder of air. The deepest part of the dive lay just ahead, and after a further 60 metres the second hand-held bottle was discarded. I was still very nervous. As I reached the previous limit at 250 metres, the fourth bottle was still untouched. The new reel was attached, and in visibility little more than one metre I moved forward. Keeping close to the right-hand wall, along which I had systematically laid the Darren Cilau line, I expected to make the connection at any minute. However, as 30 then 40 metres of line was trailed out, I became increasingly worried. Was I really in the correct passage? Perhaps this wasn't the way to Darren at all but rather a parallel route leading to Aggy. Tension was mounting. I was desperately close to my safety margin. Very shortly I would be forced to turn back. My eyes were frantically searching that critical area along the foot of the wall, craving for deliverance. I cursed myself again for not having laid a brightly-coloured line in Darren. I had installed reasonably conspicuous white line for nearly 300 metres but in the process of preparing the reel to be used on the last push I'd topped up the white cord with about 40 metres of scrap green line— possibly the most difficult colour of all to spot in murky water!

Suddenly, at the moment of despair, I arrived smack on the end of the Darren line. I'd made the link! There was no sense of jubilation, only incredible relief that I had to go no further. The line was immediately tied off. I then abandoned the reel

A camp scene during the HTV film shoot in Darren Cilau. Andy Cave (left) and Angela Garwood (right with red hat—now Mrs Cave) of the Rock Steady Crew prepare an evening meal. This camp was established in the Big Chamber Nowhere Near The Entrance.

and, in visibility close to zero, I headed back. The return journey, however, was no less tense. Fine silt obscured everything. I groped back down the tunnel retrieving the two stage bottles as I went. By the time I passed the Corner I should have relaxed, but I couldn't. I dropped one of the stage bottles and moved on quickly.

No sooner had I left the main tunnel and started along the 40 metre rift to Elm Hole than I was beset by a fresh set of problems. The line caught in the buckle of my fin strap, twice in the space of 10 metres. And judging by the reduced orange 'glow' in front of my mask, one light had run out. In the horrendous visibility thereafter, obstruction after obstruction 'appeared' in rapid succession. It was as though the cave was trying to exact some form of revenge for my earlier success. By the time I reached the squeeze at the foot of the final ascent I knew that both air bottles were severely depleted.

As I wriggled frantically up between the walls I got caught yet again. By now I was breathing very heavily. A surging silvery mass mushroomed into the space around my mask. The regular muffled rumble was replaced by a thunderous roar. Thoughts of dumping the offending fin were quickly ruled out. I simply couldn't reach down to prize it free. With my head up in the tightest section there was no room to exchange mouthpieces either. Other than cut the line, the only option was to try and pull myself forward for a metre or so. Mustering all my strength and control I heaved myself up and gained that essential room to manoeuvre. The line was freed.

A cold, shaken diver bobbed back to the surface after a lapse of 46 minutes. The lads were all there: Huw Durban, Robert Hughes, Graham Martin and Gareth Walker. Stewart Baggs took a photo and the tale was related. The first connection had been achieved. A little over 45 metres of new line had been laid out and the 295 metre line from the Elm Hole base had been tied in to the end of the Darren Cilau line. The outcome had been successful and I was very, very glad that it was all over.

Supported by Arthur Millett, John Cooper and a host of others, a solo through trip from Darren Cilau to Elm Hole was undertaken on Monday, 11 August 1986. The preparations for the dive and the departure were filmed live and featured as part of an HTV documentary. The 625 metre dive was to use four cylinders and take 50 minutes, whilst the entire journey through the system took seven and three quarter hours. On a personal level, it had been one of my lifetime's ambitions to have achieved this first traverse of the mountain; in the context of the United Kingdom the undertaking was both the longest—4.8 kilometres (three miles)—and the deepest (213 metres) subterranean journey between two caves.

In the meantime, Ian Rolland had developed a keen interest in the upstream passages beyond St David's Sump. In November 1985 he and the late Rob Parker made a most audacious exploration when they negotiated a constricted crawlway close to the Gloom Room. They had already spent over seven hours under-ground before they set off into the uninspiring side lead. Pushing sand into the sides of a flat-out crawlway required considerable dedication. But their perseverance paid off. One and a half hours later they had covered over a mile of new cave. A very real feeling of isolation crept over them; this was unquestionably the most isolated place in any British cave. They named it the Seventh Hour Sump.

They turned around and quietly retraced their steps. High above their heads several tantalising openings were noted, and within a very short distance they gained access to a prominent side passage in the left-hand wall. Around the very first corner they found themselves confronted by a fabulous grotto, fine recompense for the depressing nature of the Borrowed Boots Streamway. Rob instantly named the cavern the Icing on the Cake.

Stewart Baggs confronts the Icing on the Cake, the formations in the side passage close to the Seventh Hour Sump. This passage is a couple of minutes from the Restaurant.

It was an exhausted but very happy pair who quietly walked into White Walls at 5.00 a.m. The 1,600 metres of passage discovered by Ian and Rob headed right into that last, large uncharted block of territory; their discovery was, quite possibly, the key to the mysteries of Eglwys Faen and the Main Passage of Agen Allwedd.

Over 2.5 kilometres of dry passage had been found beyond St David's Sump, a strategically placed network which, due to its extreme isolation, had yet to be fully explored. There were any number of small passages, new digs and climbs waiting to be tackled in this area, any one of which might prove to be the exciting link with Agen Allwedd or Eglwys Faen.

Cameraman Sid Perou filming in the constricted entrance passage of Darren Cilau.

The End in Sight?

The ultimate goal was a 'dry' link-up of the major caves, an aim firmly set in the sights of the more determined cavers. The most significant work at this time was to be undertaken by a group of friends from the Cardiff and Bristol area—Steve Allen, Pete Bolt, Andy Cave and Mark Lumley, who styled themselves the Rock Steady Crew. Their operational base was situated about 300 metres up the King's Road, almost as far from the surface as was humanly possible without resorting to diving. They named their base Hard Rock Cafe. Here was a lead, a passage largely blocked by coarse sand and sporting a very slight draught. In view of the passage's encouraging trend, and the extensive network that now lay beyond the upstream St David's Sump, it was certainly worth attempting an all out assault.

From an excavational point of view the main difficulty was the fact that the dig lay 3.6 kilometres (two and a quarter miles) from the surface and involved four or more gruelling hours of caving before any work could begin. Indeed, the team soon realised that in order to accomplish the task they needed to adopt a 'backyard expedition' approach. A base was established and this was slowly equipped with a full complement of camp gear, thereby gradually reducing the feeling of remoteness. It was Steve Allen who was instrumental in setting up a major camp at Hard Rock Cafe in 1986 and the following extract from his diary recalls the atmosphere during one of their long duration stays:

> 10.00 p.m. and there's movement in the oxbow off the Kings Road. A brief bout of coughing ensues, and an electric lamp is switched on while someone searches for a light for the 'bedside' candle. In the dim illumination others stir and enquire of the time. Upon receiving a reply, one or two groan and retreat further into their sleeping bags while others—oppressed by the call of nature—clamber out of their pits and head for the loo. Those in comfortable thermal clothing just slip on their wellies or boots, while those with wetsuits contemplate the hideous routine of changing into cold, damp gear.
>
> An hour later the music is playing and the food is almost ready. Lights appear in the distance as the 'day shift' arrive back at camp after the long sandy, sometimes strenuous journey to the distant passage 'end'. They report their progress to the fresh team, and write entries in the camp log-book as those in 'morning' mode polish off breakfast and collect their gear for a 10 hour trip up the Hard Rock Extensions.
>
> In another two hours the Hard Rock Cafe will once more fall silent as the cavers settle down to some well-earned sleep. Eight hours later the process will be repeated—only the roles will have reversed.

The committment and hard work was to pay off. By the autumn of 1986 the Rock Steady Crew had opened up over 1.5 kilometres of passage towards the Divers' Extensions.

At the end of August 1987, Ian Rolland accompanied by Rick Stanton, a northern caver he had met on an expedition in Peru, mounted another trip to his recently found extensions in Darren Cilau. It was an uneventful trip down through the cave, but at the furthest point Ian made a bold and demanding climb beyond which the pair discovered another tremendously exciting extension—terminating at a deep shaft. They decided to call their new series Agua Colorada, after the base camp where they had met in Peru. The new chamber was named La Plaza—the Meeting Place. They also found a small but fabulous grotto named Cordillera Blanca. Within this section were stalactites and stalagmites in profusion, but the crowning glory was a dense interwoven display of helictites—a glorious confusion of pure, glistening, white calcite. For several minutes they stood and pondered the sight that lay before them. Here, in splendid isolation and seclusion, they had stumbled upon perhaps the finest, most exquisite set of formations under the mountain. Furthermore, they now had an extremely promising lead, one that promised to take them well on the way towards a connection with Agen Allwedd, or Eglwys Faen.

The journey out was gruelling. They passed the sump uneventfully, and were thankful of a meal at the Divers' Camp, close to Hard Rock Cafe. They then set out on the last leg.

'Pausing for Rick to get through the low section in Eglwys Passage I glanced at my watch: it was 6.20 a.m. The next thing I knew,' recalls Ian, 'was Rick calling me. I had fallen asleep and he had come back to find me.'

A total of twenty-one hours elapsed before they finally crawled out of the entrance. Skin rubbed raw, bruised and desperately tired, the journey out had taken them the best part of nine hours!

Ian Rolland and Rick Stanton were joined by Steve Jones for the continuation of the exploration scheduled for 3 October 1987. A fast and efficient team of sherpas helped them up to St David's Sump, but from there on they were on their own. An arduous journey lay ahead. On previous trips they had found to their cost that wetsuits, when worn for any length of time, produced very painful rub marks. This trip was going to be even longer, so, once beyond the sump, they changed into 'dry gear'. Then, equipped with containers of food, a stove, rope and rudimentary climbing gear, they set off through the cave.

At the climb—now named Jacob's Ladder—they filled a container with water and carried it up into the huge barren waste of La Plaza. The sense of isolation at this remote location was extreme. To counter the psychological stress and boost morale, the three decided to prepare a brew of tea. As their few spartan provisions were laid out on a flat rock and the gas stove started to purr, Ian christened the spot the Restaurant at the end of the Universe. Like mountaineers facing a long drawn out siege assault on a major mountain peak, they established a small depot, the value of which was more psychological than real. The brief rest, however, had been invaluable, and revitalised by the hot, sweet brew they were soon on their way.

Spirits were high as the new pitch was rigged and one by one they abseiled into the depths. They had reached their goal. Beyond lay virgin territory. A gypsum encrusted crawlway soon gave way to a spacious passage, the Inca Trail. Tacky mud stuck to the soles of their wellies and occasionally the route forced them to dig through localised, collapsed sections. However, the exploration was not as easy as they might have wished, for time was running out. About 400 metres from the Big Chamber, Ian led them through yet another excavation. Regrouping, they sat down for a momentary rest. Suddenly, with an almighty thud, a moderate-size boulder detached itself from the roof a couple of metres away. One of them must have accidentally brushed against it. Eyes flashed from one to the other. It was not unusual for the odd rock to move or settle while exploring or passing a choke but when one separated from an otherwise stable roof, it was a little eerie and somewhat unnerving. They topped up with carbide and in so doing the water situation was discussed. By now their meagre supply had run out. Surprisingly, not so much as a drip had been seen since the Seventh Hour Sump and if a supply didn't turn up within an hour they would have to turn back. As Ian relates, there was only one solution to their predicament:

> My carbide light was now completely out of water; I had to force my dehydrated body to have a pee. [Without water their lamps would not function; in an emergency urine can be used as a substitute.] Rick said he would join me. I could only manage an egg-cup full but Rick was in full spate. He offered to fill up my generator as well. He held tight and I passed it over for him to hold . . . but as luck would have it the interruption was such that he was unable to start up again!

Weary and thirsty they set off once more.

A little over 500 metres from the Big Chamber they entered another chamber. By now all were feeling extremely tired. They slumped onto a convenient rock and gratefully consumed their last piece of chocolate, a Starbar. They assessed the chamber from a sitting position. All were agreed they had done enough.

Ian, Rick and Steve returned to their 'Restaurant' after six hours; it

Rick Stanton abseiling into the large chamber beyond La Plaza on the day of the breakthrough to Friday the Thirteenth Passage

93

was 3.00 a.m. and they had been underground for 16 hours. Water was soon on the boil and a hot meal quickly prepared. They were aware that it would take, at the very least, seven hours to reach the surface, probably considerably longer in view of their fatigue. It was therefore decided that they should have a sleep before starting on the long journey out and, in an attempt to escape the cooling draught, they adjourned to the neighbouring Balzas Chamber. 'With Steve in the middle,' recalls Ian, 'the three of us huddled together in a pathetic attempt to keep warm. After only 45 minutes of dozing our shivering became too much.'

There were no further options: they had to start on the long trek out, a painfully tiring exit. By the time they finally reached the light of day at the Darren entrance, they had been underground for a total of 26 hours. They had discovered another kilometre of cave and had located further leads to pursue. They would have to return, yet again!

Conducting a radio location exercise on the moor above Darren Cilau: From left to right: Steve Allen, Stuart France and Bill Gascoine.

While cavers at large stood in awe of the advance, Ian was making plans. As they had extended the cave to the very limit of human endurance, the next time would involve establishing a camp in La Plaza. There was no problem getting the necessary gear through the sump or carrying it on to the camp. All that was needed was time, probably the best part of a week for anything significant and worthwhile to be achieved. It was deemed that three people would be perfectly adequate for the operation that Ian had in mind and, as Steve declined the invitation, I found myself co-opted. The plans went ahead and the date was set: Ian and Rick had earmarked the week commencing Monday, 9 November 1987.

On 17 October there was a sudden and totally unexpected development. The Rock Steady Crew broke through their long-term dig: some 21 months after they had started the dig in the King's Road they were through to the Divers' Extensions—the section of passage discovered by Rob and Ian in November 1985, now named Borrowed

94

Boots Streamway. This advance came as a big morale booster. The diggers were now within an ace of gaining the front line. The isolated Divers' Extensions, with all the scope that the site so clearly offered, would soon be open to all.

The 'diggers' new route down into the streamway was via an extremely tight and intimidating squeeze. This was impossible to tackle in a straightforward vertical direction and was only just passable by wriggling along sideways near roof level. Even here the width of the gap was considerably less than eight inches and any slip could easily spell disaster. They named the squeeze the Micron.

As far as we 'divers' were concerned this was a very timely development. Provided that we were capable of squeezing through the Micron, it meant that at least two hours carrying time would be saved. The three of us in question were well used to tight spots, and even though there was an element of uncertainty involved in this choice of route, it had to be worth an attempt. If anyone failed to pass the Micron, they could always return to the original route—as planned at the outset— and dive through St David's Sump.

The final plan was that Ian and Rick would enter the cave on Tuesday; I would join them two days later. From the start the sheer volume of material to be transported was a real headache and it was a slightly apprehensive pair who set off into the cave. By the time they reached the dreaded squeeze they were pushing and pulling five loads apiece. Dripping with perspiration, they were, by now, quite adamant that even if they could not get their bodies through the Micron they would manage to squeeze the majority of the loads down through the fissure. But, following the detailed instructions given by Andy Cave, both passed the obstacle without too much trouble. However, it was gone 10.00 p.m. before they reached La Plaza, the site of their intended base. Ten hours after entry they were fed, watered and bedded down for the night.

Ian Rolland reflecting on a successful day's exploration at the first long-duration camp at the Restaurant At The End Of The Universe, La Plaza, in November 1987.

Ian Rolland peers from the comfort of his sleeping bag in the camp established in November 1987.

My diary relates the subsequent events:

By the time I arrived on Thursday afternoon the pair had completed the main climbing objectives. Clearly, the resulting 200 metres of passage was disappointing; they had been hoping for much better things. The main area of promise now was the back end of the Agua Colorada Series, the really exciting area nearest to Aggy. They had deliberately postponed the examination of this section until my arrival.

Friday morning arrived. We breakfasted on lumpy custard, dried fruit, Muesli cereal and vitamin pills. In the unlikely event that any of the Rock Steady Crew should also turn up, Ian scrawled out a brief note and left it prominently on top of the stove. By 11.00 a.m. we were on our way. We abseiled into the Big Chamber and about 45 minutes later Rick and I started burrowing along a low sand-filled tunnel at the previous limit of exploration. No sooner had we arrived than Ian realised that he had forgotten the survey gear. So optimistic was he that it would be required, he dutifully returned all the way back to camp to collect the vital equipment! His judgement was soon confirmed and by the time our lathered friend returned, we were sitting patiently at the start of a wide open passage, Soft Rock Cruise.

Ignoring the side leads, we moved on along a comfortable sized sandy-floored tubeway. Gradually we were forced onto our stomachs, and then the burrowing resumed. Fortunately, the dry sand was easily pushed aside by hand. Eventually we broke free.

The passage that now confronted us was over six metres high by four metres wide. Ian's compass gave a bearing of due west . . . it was running directly towards Aggy. The excitement was electrifying and, bearing in mind the date of this momentous advance, November 13th, agreement was unanimous as to the naming of this significant find. In the case of Llangattock Mountain, 'Friday the Thirteenth' would henceforth be synonymous with memories of very good luck. With beaming faces we virtually ran off down the passage.

'This is why I came on a six-day camping expedition,' said Ian.

'This is why I decided to join you,' I replied.

But all good things come to an end: 300 metres of large, trunk passage brought us to a sudden dip in the roof, and yet another sand dig. A narrow side rift took us on a further 80 metres but eventually this became too constricted for comfort. It was 10.00 p.m. before we returned to camp and there was little doubt in anyone's mind that it had been a most rewarding day. The survey was soon plotted and indicated that our furthest point was somewhere close to the end of Priory Road, at the downstream terminus in Agen Allwedd, and the end of Trident Passage, off the Main Passage.

The next day we set off to explore the two most promising leads. Although a considerable amount of passage was found the real prospects were long term. We paused for a bite to eat and drink, and conversation inevitably centred upon the number of good digs we had found. Despite the day's lack of real success, spirits were high. Ian flippantly suggested that we ought to auction the best sites:

'The Warren: what am I bid for this promising dig? . . . Do I hear £50 from Mr Gardener? I have £60 from Mr Millett . . . No, no . . . £100 from the Rock Steady Crew.'

Tears began to form in our eyes. We were crying with laughter. Ian went on:

'Dig with strong draught—has potential. Come on, ladies and gentlemen . . . yes, yes, £250 . . . sold to Mr Gardener!'

Rick Stanton stops to view the snow-like deposits on the floor of the Inca Trail.

Ian Rolland negotiating one of the sand digs, leading to Friday the Thirteenth Passage.

Andy Cave of the Rock Steady Crew admires the superb formations in Cordillera Blanca Chamber, a short distance beyond the Restaurant.

Peter Bolt of the Rock Steady Crew examines the Blue Greenies, the copper-coloured helictites close to the Restaurant.

It was 9.00 p.m. before we arrived back in camp. Ian had arrived a little ahead of Rick and I, so while we two fixed ourselves a much needed 'electrolyte' drink, Ian raced off to check out one last area, that section downstream of the camp but in the upper levels.

About 15 minutes later an excited figure came racing back:

'Just found this three-metre square passage heading off into the distance . . . fabulous grottos as well.'

Rick's feet were in a very bad way. For two days he had been suffering with blisters, which by now had been rubbed raw by continual movement. But such was the level of Ian's excitement it would have been unthinkable not to have gone along. We quickly grabbed a bite to eat, gathered together a fresh supply of carbide and water, and in minutes we were off. We were leaving the cave tomorrow; we couldn't leave a lead like this wide open.

Ian led us through the Sleeping Chamber and along a short length of narrow rift, when suddenly we popped up into another spacious section of trunk passage, the Divers' Last Stand. Here, as Ian had related, there was a fabulous grotto [Blue Greenies] on a par with that in Cordillera Blanca Chamber; certainly one of the finest in the British Isles. The draught led us on for several hundred metres but when the passage degenerated into a constricted jagged rift, we had had enough. Rick's feet were giving him agony, and we had seen much bigger and better decorated passage some way back.

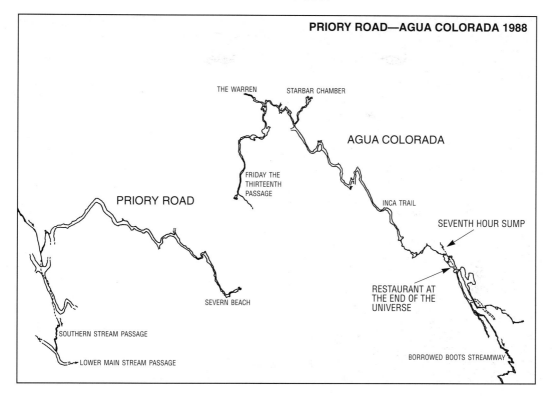

PRIORY ROAD—AGUA COLORADA 1988

THE WARREN   STARBAR CHAMBER

AGUA COLORADA

FRIDAY THE THIRTEENTH PASSAGE

PRIORY ROAD

INCA TRAIL

SEVENTH HOUR SUMP

RESTAURANT AT THE END OF THE UNIVERSE

SEVERN BEACH

SOUTHERN STREAM PASSAGE

LOWER MAIN STREAM PASSAGE

BORROWED BOOTS STREAMWAY

It was 1.00 a.m. when we returned to camp and 2.30 a.m. when we changed for the night. With a full stomach and snuggled comfortably in the warmth of our bags, the aches and pains melted away. As the last light was extinguished thoughts turned inward. What a day it had turned out to be; what a fantastic introduction to camping in the cave.

The next morning three weary bodies packed away their gear, cleaned up the camp and set off out. The six-day camp had yielded 1,500 metres of new passage and many more digs. Agua Colorada was now 2.7 kilometres (1.7 miles) in length and all was set, or so it seemed, for an imminent connection with either Priory Road or Trident Passage in Agen Allwedd. But perhaps the most exciting outcome of the exploration was the fact that the whole of Darren Cilau was now open to all.

Underwater excavations at Pwll y Cwm rising. The diver is Steve Ainley. Graham Martin and Gareth Walker pull up a container full of stones.

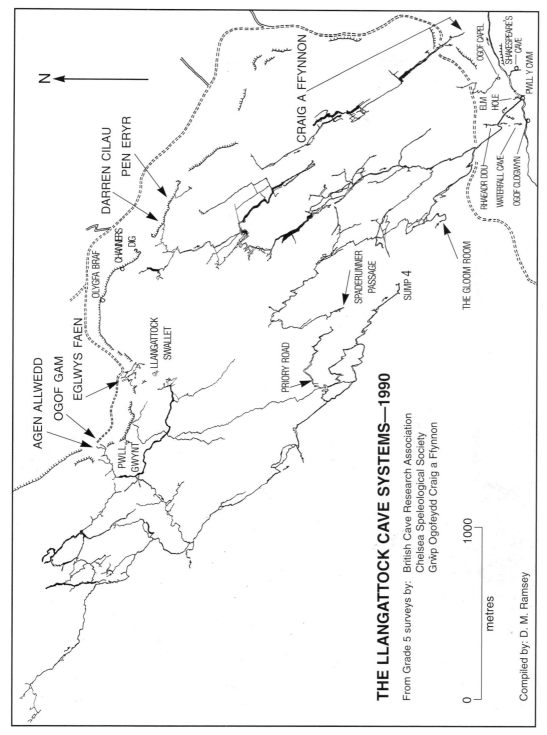

CRAIG A FFYNNON

DARREN CILAU
PEN ERYR

OGOF CAPEL
SHAKESPEARE'S
CAVE
PWLL Y CWM
ELM HOLE
RHAEADR DDU
WATERFALL CAVE
OGOF CLOGWYN

CHAMBER
DIG

OLYGFA BRAF

EGLWYS FAEN

AGEN ALLWEDD
OGOF GAM

LLANGATTOCK
SWALLET

PWLL
GWYNT

SPADERUNNER
PASSAGE
SUMP 4

PRIORY ROAD

THE GLOOM ROOM

THE LLANGATTOCK CAVE SYSTEMS—1990

From Grade 5 surveys by: British Cave Research Association
Chelsea Speleological Society
Grŵp Ogofeydd Craig a Ffynnon

Compiled by: D. M. Ramsey

0   1000
metres

So Near yet So Far: Future Possibilities

Optimism regarding a quick connection with Agen Allwedd soon evaporated. Within weeks of the 'divers' last camp, the Rock Steady Crew advanced their base of operations to the Restaurant, above Jacob's Ladder, and the team settled back into 'siege mode'. Following two lucky breaks in February 1989 (600 metres) and August 1990 (200 metres), the gap between Darren Cilau and Agen Allwedd was whittled down from 250 metres to 60 metres. The closest point between the two systems now lay somewhere in the vicinity of the furthest dry terminus in Darren and at the very end of the remote Priory Road Passage, in the downstream sector of Agen Allwedd. But, as so often happens, the impetus in Darren Cilau had already begun to wane.

Very few cavers had the time at their disposal to join any prolonged assault at the end of Darren; to achieve anything, a three-day or longer mission was necessary. With six kilometres to travel before it became possible to explore for new ground, or dig for a connection, it was not surprising that some groups were taking a fresh look at other sites rather nearer to the surface. It was the 1987 Gloucester Spelaeological Society's extensions at the end of Priory Road that drew my attention. The terminal area here was only four kilometres and three hours from the entrance. If a connection could be established at this point, the outcome would be a 10 kilometre through trip, arguably rating among the top three trips in the world. This was a goal well worth striving to attain.

Tony Donovan in the process of pushing out a container of sand from the dig in the Bunker.

Tony Donovan and 'Spike' working the bellows in the Bunker at the end of Priory Road. Due to the lack of any air flow, breathing in 'dead end' tunnels is well nigh impossible. Bellows are used in an attempt to aerate the passages.

Jason and Tony Donovan, and a wealth of essential equipment, in Sick Parrot Chamber, a few metres from the excavations in the Mother Of All Battles and the Bunker, 1991.

A large support team carry scaffold poles into Agen Allwedd to support the roof in the Mother Of All Battles Choke, summer 1991.

Despite the tedious nature of the notorious Southern Stream Passage, the terminal area of Priory Road was to become a contender for the most concerted digging effort witnessed in the cave. Early in 1991 a short extension reduced the gap to 40 metres. Radio communication between the caves was achieved and this, together with an electronic location exercise, provided further information regarding relative alignment and proximity. But, despite a determined effort on three separate fronts, hopes of achieving a link faded in the summer of 1992 . . . a mere 15 metres short of success!

Other groups were also working in areas that might ultimately lead to a connection between Agen Allwedd and Darren Cilau, but as 1992 gave way to 1993 there was only one small group that seemed to be in with a real chance of success, namely the cave divers. It was to be Duncan Price and Rick Stanton who were to take up the gauntlet and, eventually, gain just rewards. By mid 1991, Duncan and Rick had made a systematic examination of the sump upstream of Elm Hole. Unfortunately, there seemed to be no direct route to Agen Allwedd from here but, between their longer dives, the pair worked at the underside of the main Pwll y Cwm blockage. Like other cave divers, they realised that a direct route into the drainage outlet, illiminating the tortures of Elm Hole, would solve a lot of problems. Trying to dig downwards through the pothole in the bed of the river Clydach had already been shown to be slow and labour intensive. However, the main tunnel beneath was substantial and it was surprising how much debris one diver, working on his own, could move. The judicious application of a crowbar to the wall of massive cobbles generated collapse after collapse and quickly caused the floor of Pwll y Cwm pothole to subside. In September 1993 success was finally achieved: a shaft was opened and future operations would access the submerged leads in Darren Cilau via the resurgence.

Taking advantage of this new route of entry, Rick passed the Gloom Room Sump in August 1994 and over the space of another two trips progressed, via two further sumps, to a massive boulder choke. He had gained over 600 metres of passage and advanced this branch of Darren Cilau to within, perhaps, 40 metres of Against All Odds Chamber at the end of Sump 4 in Agen Allwedd.

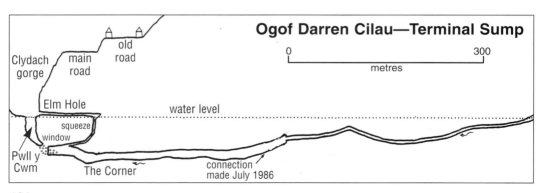

Ogof Darren Cilau—Terminal Sump

104

That the caves of Llangattock will eventually link up is no longer a matter of debate; the burning concern is where will this be achieved. In the fullness of time, doubtless there will be several points of connection and in the process many kilometres of new passage will be revealed. But as is so often the case, luck plays a very important part in cave exploration. In March 1993, for example, our team transferred their energies from the Agen Allwedd-Darren Cilau link to a connection with Craig a Ffynnon. In the space of a few trips the choke at the end of Antler Passage (off Epocalypse Passage) was passed, well over 1.5 kilometres of passage had been revealed and the gap in this area was reduced to less than 75 metres. How ironic that we had just concluded two years of work in Agen Allwedd for a mere 120 metres!

Busmans Holiday Passage, a mile long extension to Darren Cilau was achieved in 1993. This takes Darren Cilau to within 75 metres of a possible connection with Ogof Craig a Ffynnon. The two cavers are Gareth Hardman (foreground) and Ben Church (background).

With each new discovery fresh leads are also revealed, sites that will undoubtedly prove challenging and exciting for future generations. The mountain, once thought to be barren of significant cave formation, has now yielded one of the longest systems in the world. Between them, the three major cave systems total well over 70 kilometres of passage. Taking all other caves into account and the strong likelihood of many more extensions and interconnections, the entire system will, in all probability, exceed 100 kilometres, or even 150 kilometres sometime in the next century!

This book has concerned itself with the exploration of the caves beneath Llangattock Mountain, the network of passages largely comprising Agen Allwedd, Craig a Ffynnon and Darren Cilau, which drain to the Clydach gorge. But it is interesting to speculate upon the fact that Llangynidr Mountain is the geographical extension of the established caving area. Both geology and hydrology hint at the existence of a major complex of undiscovered passages beneath the adjoining moors. Likewise, in the mid sector of the mountain, particularly in that enigmatic area surrounding Eglwys Faen, a labyrinth of interconnected passages can assuredly be postulated extending between, and connecting with, Agen Allwedd and Darren Cilau.

Close to Ogof Craig a Ffynnon, there is another discreet little entrance below the site of the old Drum and Monkey public house, namely Ogof Capel. Following Bill Gascoine's successful water trace from Eglwys Faen to this particular resurgence,

Steve Ainley prepares to dive in Ogof Capel, in the Clydach gorge.

Dig Hastilow in the profusely decorated Ogof Capel, a site now threatened with closure due to proposed road improvements in the Clydach gorge.

digging efforts were rewarded in the summer of 1987. A determined effort on the part of Steve Ainley and Gareth Cooper led them through a formidable boulder choke and into a spectacularly decorated length of streamway. This has revealed nearly a kilometre of passage and gives further credance to the existence of an intricate web of interconnecting passageways running the length and breadth of the mountain.

Dye testing has played a crucial role in our understanding of the area's caving potential and it is now known that a vast sector of Llangynidr Mountain drains to Ffynnon Gisfaen, the large spring situated at the head of the Clydach gorge. The geography of the network is poorly understood but it would seem that the catchment area of two systems overlap. The system of caves described in this book occupies the lower limestone beds of Llangattock Mountain, whilst the Gisfaen drainage network occupies the upper beds. If one thinks of the rock strata as being analogous to a two-storey house then, quite simply, we have, so far, merely explored the ground floor. We have yet to discover what lies upstairs.

The long hypothesized cave system associated with Ffynnon Gisfaen has a catchment extending well over eight kilometres to the west—encompassing Ogof Gynnes and, perhaps, the famous Chartist Cave. It was in the summer of 1991 that the key to this system was finally revealed. Following a lengthy digging operation by Brynmawr Caving Club, at a point 1,800 metres from the entrance to a man-made adit, the Carno cave system was extended to over 9 kilometres in length.

Steve Pedrazzoli in the Carno Adit, a man made tunnel driven into Llangynidr Mt. from Rassau, at the head of the Ebbw Vale valley. This tunnel was planned as a water conduit intending to take water from the Cleisfer valley to the north to the industrial area in the south. Although it failed to reach its goal the tunnel did intercept natural cave passage—the lengthy, complex Carno Cave System.

Over two hours from the entrance, the late Brian Murliss negotiates a typically unpleasant section—aptly named Southern Discomfort—of the Carno cave system.

A glance at the map of Llangattock Mountain gives a very clear indication of the vast potential still waiting to be realised. And given the close proximity of the two hydrological systems, it begs the question as to whether the Carno system links up with the network at Llangattock?

The possibility of any lengthy cave network being found at Llangattock was met with ridicule as late as 1950. That such an extensive complex of caves should exist beneath the bleak, featureless moors of Llangattock and Llangynidr seems hard to believe. While still fragmented and with several important connections between caves yet to be discovered, few would dispute the fact that the Llangattock cave system is, in reality, one vast labyrinth. It is possibly the longest continuous dry network in the British Isles. However, the mountain has been slow to divulge its secrets and without doubt there is still much to learn. But what we have learned has certainly shed new light upon the secrets of adjoining mountain areas. In 1994, for example, Gilwern Hill and the Blorenge, the hill masses south of the Clydach gorge divulged the immense labyrinth Ogof Ddraenen. At the time of publication, this system is the prime contender for the status of the longest cave in the British Isles. Within the space of two years, the miniscule hole at Pwll Du was transformed from a squirm-hole less than 30 metres in length to a network well over 50 kilometres in extent! As with the caves beneath Llangattock Mountain and Llangynidr Mountain, it will take many years before the exploration of this system is complete.

Our caves represent one of the last true wilderness areas on Earth. Other than Eglwys Faen, which has in the past suffered at the hands of uncaring and ill-informed visitors, the vast proportion of caves have suffered little human impact. They are substantially as they were when they were first discovered. In many ways it is extremely fortuitous that the caves have only been revealed in recent times. Ogof Agen Allwedd did not reach the limelight until 1958, by which time the environmental movement was well established. Indeed, the entrances to both Eglwys Faen and Agen Allwedd already lay within the designated Craig y Cilau Reserve, a National Nature Reserve established in October 1959. In recognition of the importance of the extensive and complex cave system, additional protection was afforded to the mountain as a whole in 1986 when the area was designated a Site of Special Scientific Interest.

Gilwern Hill, from the Llangattock-Bryn-mawr tramroad, where spectacular caving discoveries have been made in Ogof Ddraenen.

Llangynidr moor: a vast amount of passage remains to be discovered beneath these pock-marked moors. Much will doubtless come to light as the Carno cave system, located beneath the two reservoirs in the distance, is explored further.

The entrance to Chartist Cave where strong draughts give a clear indication of the tremendous exploratory potential of Llangynidr Mountain.

From the outset, cavers have been actively involved in conservational issues. Llangattock Mountain is host to wonderful treasures and is in need of special protection. The entrance to Agen Allwedd (more precisely Ogof Gam) was gated and locked in 1960, and a system of access implemented which has successfully stood the test of time. With its 'log-book' inside the entrance, it has been possible to monitor visitors and influence the pattern of cave usage, a situation without parallel anywhere in the United Kingdom. It has transpired that about 1,000 people visit the cave annually, a figure that has remained constant since 1960. Ogof Craig a Ffynnon is also gated but access to Darren Cilau is unrestricted; its conservation relies upon the extreme nature of the entrance passage and the responsibility of visiting cavers.

Cave conservation is of paramount importance. It is incumbent upon us all to minimise our impact on the underground environment. While it may be an environment sculpted from solid rock, it is, in many respects, a fragile and vulnerable world. The public readily appreciate the susceptibility of a stalactite straw to damage or destruction but the impact of human activity on cave life, for example, is less apparent. People often enquire as to whether anything lives in the caves. The simple answer is 'yes' but as most of the true cave fauna is microscopic in size its existence is not obvious to the casual visitor. Bats, however, are frequent visitors at certain times of the year and occasionally these have been found several kilometres from the nearest entrance. Eight of the fifteen British species have been recorded in the Llangattock caves, although the rare Lesser Horseshoe is the most abundant. Agen Allwedd has several important bat roosts, notably close to the First Boulder Choke. Here the annual temperature range fluctuates between 6.5° to 7.8°C and between November and April the site may be home to as many as 200 bats, making the cave the most important place of hibernation for the lesser horseshoe in Britain, and one of the most important in Europe. As a consequence, many underground activities cease, or are restricted, during the winter months. Whilst bat populations may be in decline nationally, cavers are modestly proud of the fact that the numbers recorded underground remain stable.

To date, no evidence has been found of human occupation in any of the caves of south-east Wales. Although bones have been recovered from the Chartist Cave on Llangynidr moor—dramatically testifying to human conflict during the early years of the industrial revolution—no remains have come to light in the caves of Llangattock. Cavers, and those excavating new entrances, will

A lesser horseshoe bat in hibernation. Bats are protected by law and to avoid disturbance certain restrictions are applied in caving activities over the winter period.

need to keep their eyes open in order to ensure that valuable archaeological finds are not passed over in the future.

We live on a shrinking planet where each and every one of us must adjust to change. This book has not only sought to present the magnificent caves of south-east Wales to the world and provide an insight to the sport of caving, but also, hopefully, to improve communication between interested parties. Caves and cavers do not exist in isolation; there must, of necessity, be liason between landowners, commoners, local residents, walkers, climbers, and authorities such as the Brecon Beacons National Park Authority and the Countryside Council for Wales, for all have a role to play in the future of the caves. The Llangattock caves have been there for millions of years; they are national 'treasures'; let us proudly proclaim their existence but let us also pass them on unspoilt to future generations.

Pouring dye into a disappearing surface stream, polluted by the carcass of a horse!

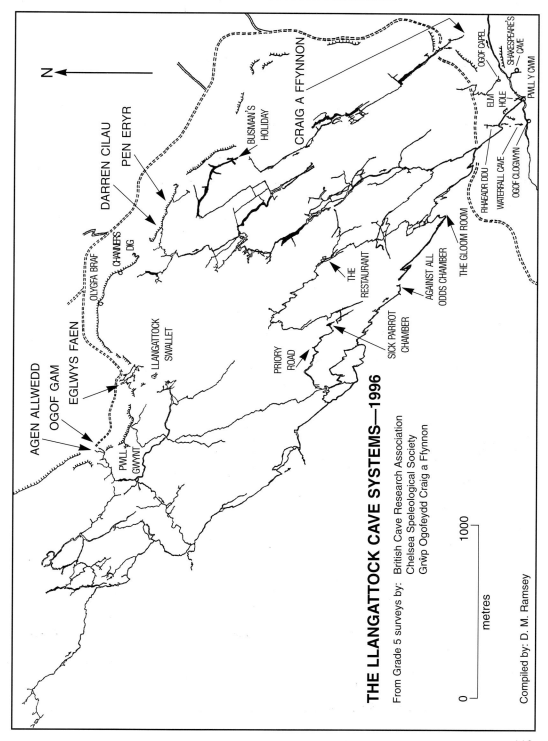

THE LLANGATTOCK CAVE SYSTEMS—1996

From Grade 5 surveys by: British Cave Research Association
Chelsea Speleological Society
Grŵp Ogofeydd Craig a Ffynnon

Compiled by: D. M. Ramsey

Appendix I

Cave exploration: a chronology

1938: Dragon Group visit Eglwys Faen.

1946: Brian Price explores Ogof Gam and discovers entrance to Ogof Agen Allwedd.

1949: Reverend Cecil Cullingford visits Blaen Onneu Caves.

1950: David Seagrave and Harold Hicken enter Agen Allwedd.

1951: Brian Price lowers the water in the ducks at the end of Ogof Gam, to make connection with Agen Allwedd; Victor Oliver and Graham Holly make first round trip.

1954: Edward Aslett, Bill Clarke and Gordon Clissold (South Wales Caving Club) dig First Boulder Choke in Agen Allwedd.
Mel Davies discovers Ogof Pen Eryr.

1956: British Nylon Spinners Spelaeological Society (B.N.S.) extend Eglwys Faen as far as New Cavern.
Chelsea Spelaeological Society (C.S.S.) climb to Guano Passage in Agen Allwedd.

1957: C.S.S. climb to Angel's Roost in Agen Allwedd.
B.N.S. discover entrance to Ogof Darren Cilau.
Hereford Caving Club (H.C.C.) pass First Boulder Choke in Agen Allwedd.

1958: H.C.C. explore most of Agen Allwedd as far as Deep Water.
June: 'Official' passage of Turkey Pool.
Nov.: C.S.S. 'record' the discovery of Third Boulder Choke.

1959: April: H.C.C. discover the Summertime Series in Agen Allwedd.
Harold Lord mounts surveying expedition.
June: First circular route achieved—The Inner Circle.
Nov.: Calcite Squeeze reached in Darren Cilau.

1960: April: Harold Lord mounts second surveying expedition in Agen Allwedd.
June: C.S.S. reach Fourth Boulder Choke.

1961: Aug.: Mel Davies proves hydrological connection between Agen Allwedd and Pwll y Cwm rising.

1962: Easter: Ken Pearce, Geoff Morgan and Bob Toogood reach Lower Main Streamway in Agen Allwedd.
Whitsun: British Spelaeological Association explore Biza Passage.

1963:   Apr.: Mike Boon and Fred Davies extend Darren Cilau to one kilometre.
Apr.: Harold Lord and C.S.S. achieve the Outer Circle Route in Agen Allwedd.
Apr.: First dive at Terminal Downstream Sump, Agen Allwedd.

1964:   Easter: Mike Jeanmaire and Colin Graham pass sump in Shakespeare's Cave.

1966:   May: Mike Wooding and John Sinclair dive Turkey Sumps, Agen Allwedd.
June: Mike Wooding and John Sinclair pass Turkey Sump 2.
Oct.: Mike Wooding and John Sinclair pass Sump 3; discover 600 metres.

1967:   Martyn Farr discovers Ogof Gynnes on Llangynidr Mountain.

1971:   Nov.: John Parker makes first dive in Turkey Sump 5, Agen Allwedd.
Dec.: John Parker and Jeff Phillips pass Sump 5 and discover 600 metres (Remembrance Series).

1972:   April: John Parker dives Terminal Downstream Sump, Agen Allwedd; enters Sump 3.
May: Eldon Pothole Club achieve connection between Biza and Fourth Choke, and establish the Grand Circle.
July: John Parker dives Terminal Downstream Sump 3 for 750 feet.

1973:   Jan.: Roger Solari and Martyn Farr extend Remembrance Series by 600 metres.

1974:   May: Martyn Farr passes Terminal Downstream Sump to discover Maytime.
June: Tragedy at Terminal Downstream Sump 4.

1976:   July: Ogof Craig a Ffynnon entered.
Nov.: Craig a Ffynnon First Choke passed.

1977:   May: Craig a Ffynnon; discovery of North West Inlet.
July: Craig a Ffynnon; Second Choke passed; Third choke passed.
Aug.: Craig a Ffynnon; discovery of Blaen Elin; discovery of Lower Series.

1978:   July: Craig a Ffynnon; Fourth Choke passed.

1981:   Mar.: C.S.S. discovery of Pwll Gwynt.
July: Terminal Downstream Sump 4 in Agen Allwedd dived to 215 metres.

1982:   Aug.: C.S.S. assault begins on Trident Passage, Agen Allwedd.

1983:   Jan.: C.S.S. reach Washout Chamber in Trident Passage, Agen Allwedd.
Feb.: Trident comes to an 'end'.
Oct.: Clive Gardener discovers Northern Streamway.

1984:   Jan.: Martyn Farr discovers 1984 Series off Shatter Passage, Agen Allwedd.
Aug.: Clive Gardener takes an interest in Darren Cilau.
Sept.: Darren Cilau breakthrough; discovery of Epocalypse, Loop Route, Eglwys Passage, etc.

1985:   Feb.: Darren Cilau; Clive Gardener and Jock Williams discover St Valentine's Series. Welly Boy Aven climbed and Tony White descends 22 metre pitch to White Passage.

Mar.: Darren Cilau; further major discoveries: Bonsai Streamway, Flyovers, Half-mile Passage, etc.

Apr.: St David's Sump passed; discovery of Psychotronic Strangeways, 1 kilometre to the Gloom Room Sump.

May: Darren Cilau; Martyn Farr commences diving in Terminal Downstream Sump. Commencement of Pwll y Cwm Cave Diving Project.

Nov.: Ian Rolland and Rob Parker discover Borrowed Boots Streamway and Seventh Hour Sump (2 kilometres).

1986:   Darren Cilau; Rock Steady Crew commence digging at head of King's Road.

Mar.: Rock Steady Crew discover Rock Steady Cruise.

Darren Cilau; third dive in Terminal Downstream Sump.

Elm Hole; Martyn Farr resumes exploration abandoned in 1974.

Apr.: Ian Rolland dives Seventh Hour Sump.

May: Rock Steady Crew reach Twelve O'Clock High.

July: Elm Hole; Martyn Farr achieves connection with Darren Cilau.

Aug.: Martyn Farr makes 625 metre through dive; Darren Cilau to Elm Hole.

Dec.: Gloucester Spelaeological Society (G.S.S.) commence digging at Gothic Passage in Agen Allwedd.

1987:   Jan.: Simultaneous breakthroughs in Gothic Passage, Agen Allwedd, by G.S.S. and C.S.S.

Feb.: Darren Cilau; Ian Rolland, Phil Rust and Steve Jones discover Saturday Night at the Movies.

Mar.: Rock Steady Crew mount a nine-day camp in Darren Cilau.

April: Rock Steady Crew push Perseverance Passage.

July: Ian Rolland passes Terminal Downstream Sump in Agen Allwedd after 291 metres.

Aug.: Darren Cilau; Ian Rolland and Rick Stanton discover Agua Colorada Series.

Oct.: Ian Rolland, Rick Stanton and Steve Jones extend Agua Colorada by another kilometre.

Rock Steady Crew extend Acupuncture Pass to the Micron and one week later discover the Divers' Extension.

Nov.: Rolland, Stanton and Farr discover Friday the Thirteenth and Painkiller (1,500 metres).

Dec.: Rock Steady Crew pass sand dig to reach boulder choke at the end of Friday the Thirteenth.

1988:   Jan.: Agen Allwedd; C.S.S. excavate a dry route to Maytime.

Mar.: Darren Cilau; Rock Steady Crew reach boulder choke in the Warren.

1989:   Feb.: Darren Cilau; Rock Steady Crew pass boulder choke at the end of Friday the Thirteenth to discover 600 metres—Still Warthogs After All These Years.

1990:   Aug.: Rock Steady Crew discover Dweebland.

1991:   Jan.: Agen Allwedd; Priory Road Choke passed to discover Sick Parrot Chamber; Aggy-Darren gap reduced to an estimated 40 metres. Major digging project initiated.
Nov.: Elm Hole; after series of dives with Rick Stanton, Duncan Price makes sump traverse to Darren and returns to Elm Hole.

1992:   Easter: Accurate (Grade 5) survey largely completed in Darren Cilau. This reveals that the separation between the two systems is only 20 metres.
The digging project is revitalised in Agen Allwedd.
May: Tony Donovan and Martyn Farr pass MOAB Choke to enter draughting passage trending towards Dweebland. Digging continues here for another six months, the gap between the two systems is narrowed to 15 metres.

1993:   A divable connection is established between Pwll y Cwm and Elm Hole.
Mar.: Darren Cilau; discovery of 1.5 kilometres in Busman's Holiday.

1994:   Diving from Pwll y Cwm; Rick Stanton and Duncan Price extend Darren by passing Gloom Room Sump.

1995:   Rick Stanton passes another sump (the second beyond the Gloom Room Sump) to take Darren to within metres of Sump 4 in Agen Allwedd.

1996:   Mar.: Agen Allwedd; sump bypass finally achieved at Turkey Sump 2.
Carno Adit; Martyn Farr mounts project at the terminal sumps: 430 metre extension downstream to Sump 5.

APPENDIX II

ACCESS ARRANGEMENTS, CONSERVATION, RESCUE

Ogof Agen Allwedd

Ogof Agen Allwedd is situated in the Craig y Cilau Nature Reserve, and access control is vested in the Mynydd Llangatwg Cave Management Advisory Committee (M.L.C.M.A.C.), who act on behalf of the Countryside Council for Wales. Entry is gained via the gated (locked) entrance at Ogof Gam. The original point of entry is also gated; no entry is possible via this route.

Keys to the cave are available to *bona-fide* caving clubs (affiliated to one of the regional caving councils) via the Permit Secretary of the Mynydd Llangatwg Cave Management Advisory Committee. A deposit of £10.00 is required, together with a stamped addressed envelope. Clubs undertaking more than four visits per year may apply to the committee for an annual permit and key, which is renewable subject to the number of trips undertaken.

The number of individuals in the party should not exceed six. The use of carbide lamps is not permitted. There are restrictions upon certain exploratory activities, and scientific studies. Applications concerning any projects of this nature will be considered by the committee. Permission is required for digging. The committee meets in early May and October. The ultimate responsibility for the management of the caves within the nature reserve—which also includes Eglwys Faen—rests with the Countryside Council for Wales.

Secretary M.L.C.M.A.C.:   Charles Bailey, 5 Old Rectory Close, Maes y Gwartha, Gilwern, Gwent NP7 ODZ
Permit Secretary: Lynne Bailey, 5 Old Rectory Close, Maes y Gwartha, Gilwern, Gwent NP7 ODZ

Ogof Craig a Ffynnon

Entry to Ogof Craig a Ffynnon is controlled by the Craig a Ffynnon Caving Group, represented upon the Mynydd Llangatwg Cave Management Advisory Committee. The cave is gated and locked and a strict 'leadership' system is operated. Maximum party size is six and all applications for entry should be made well in advance to: Jeff Hill, 11 York Avenue, Garden City, Ebbw Vale, Gwent. A stamped addressed envelope should accompany applications. The use of carbide lamps is not permitted.

Ogof Darren Cilau

At the present time there is unrestricted access to Ogof Darren Cilau and no other restrictions apply. The use of electric lighting is encouraged. Owing to the extreme nature of the entrance series a wet suit is strongly advised. N.B. Other than in the case of minor injuries, the evacuation of a casualty from this system would present the rescue organisations with **severe** difficulty.

Eglwys Faen and Ogof Pen Eryr

Eglwys Faen lies within the Craig y Cilau Nature Reserve and certain restrictions apply to exploratory activities. This is the best suited cave in the area for beginners. Although the impressive Main Chamber can be viewed by the casual rambler walking the tramroad, it is stressed that caving can be dangerous, especially for the inexperienced or the ill-equipped. For this reason, cavers visiting the site should be properly equipped and led by a suitably experienced or qualified party leader.

Ogof Pen Eryr: The entrance to this cave lies in the same quarry as Ogof Darren Cilau, but about 250 metres to the east. No restrictions apply. It is a suitable cave for beginners—no serious difficulties or hazards—but it does commence with a fairly tight squeeze!

Advice to Beginners
If you are thinking of trying the sport for the first time, contact one of the recognised trainers or outdoor centres in the area. They will direct you to an individual or organisation who can meet your needs.

If you think that you would like to pursue the activity further you are advised to join a reputable club. Your initial caving contact can generally provide advice on this matter.

Finally, all visitors are reminded to be courteous to landowners and local residents. Park your vehicle with consideration for others and follow the principles of the country code at all times. This will ensure continued access for future generations.

CONSERVATION

The Llangattock cave system is unique. Whilst every effort has been made to minimize the imposition of restrictions upon visiting cavers, the future welfare of the network is of paramount importance. The responsibility for this falls not only upon the controlling bodies and the Mynydd Llangatwg Cave Management Advisory Committee but also, to very large measure, upon the individual caver. Every precaution should be taken to avoid accidental damage. Many of the features are protected by 'tapes' and all cavers should keep to established paths. The guiding aim should be to leave the cave as one finds it. This means the removal of all waste and care for the environment as a whole. Although tolerated in Darren Cilau, the use of carbide is generally frowned upon and is banned in both Agen Allwedd and Craig a Ffynnon; electric lighting is strongly recommended in all the caves of the area.

Bats, including the rare lesser horseshoe species, hibernate in the caves during winter months. All bats are protected by the Wildlife and Countryside Act 1981 and it is illegal intentionally to kill, injure or take any bat; to disturb roosting bats; or to damage, destroy or obstruct any place used by bats for roosting. Cavers are therefore advised:

> not to handle bats, and to take extreme care not to dislodge them while passing through low passageways;
> not to photograph roosting bats;
> not to linger in areas where bats are hibernating or shine bright lights upon them. Body heat and lighting can be sufficient to awaken bats;
> noise should be kept to an absolute minimum.

ACCIDENTS AND RESCUE

Accidents don't just happen, they are caused. In view of the complex nature of much of the system, and the sheer extent of the network, cavers should reflect very carefully upon the following points:

1 Before venturing underground leave precise word regarding the cave visited, the anticipated route and the expected time of return. These details should be left with someone acquainted with cave rescue call-out procedure.

2 Consider the weather—parts of the system are impassable after heavy or prolonged rain.

3 The trip should be conducted in a sensible-sized party; to avoid getting lost and to maintain control, the leader should ensure that all personnel remain together at all times.

4 All equipment should be serviceable; spare lighting, food and basic first-aid should be carried.

5 The leader should check any 'fixed equipment' and belays found in the caves. Safety is paramount and suspect equipment should be reported to the secretary of the management committee. (The Mynydd Llangatwg Cave Management Advisory Committee accepts no responsibility for any fixed aids which may be encountered in the system.) Lifelines must be adopted on all pitches.

6 Treat all boulder chokes with caution.

7 The leader of each party should be aware of the rescue procedure existing in the area. Self rescue is encouraged but in the event of a call-out contact the police and ask for 'Cave Rescue'.

Rescue from the depths of the Llangattock system is a major undertaking. Rescue from Darren Cilau may be impossible!

A GLOSSARY OF CAVING TERMS

Abseil: A method of descending vertical rock utilising a hand-held friction device on a rope.

Active cave: A cave with a flowing stream.

Bed: A layer or stratum in a sequence of sedimentary rock.

Bedding plane: A separation line between two layers or beds of sedimentary rock: produces a characteristic wide, low-roofed passage.

Bivouac: A temporary camp in a long-distance cave expedition.

Boulder choke: A pile of rocks or boulders, as from a collapsed roof, often blocking further passage.

Calcite: Calcium carbonate in crystalline form, the main constituent of limestone.

Carbide lamp: A lamp lit by burning acetylene gas, produced by the action of water on calcium carbide.

Chimney: A narrow, vertical or steeply-inclined fissure.

Chockstone: A rock wedged in a crack; can be used for assistance, as in climbing, or as a physical support, e.g. in a boulder choke.

Column: A pillar-like formation linking cave roof and floor, usually the product of the union of a stalactite and stalagmite.

Crawl: A low passage through which progress can only be made on hands and knees, or flat-out.

Curtain: A thin, fluted sheet or draping of dripstone; sometimes a row or group of regularly-shaped stalactites.

Dig: An excavation above or below ground to find a new cave or section of cave.

Dip: The inclination of a bed of rock, its angle from the horizontal being expressed in degrees. It is measured by a clinometer.

Doline: Surface hollow caused by solution of limestone or the collapse of an underground cave.

Duck: A point where the roof slopes to meet the water level or where there is little air space, which is traversed by a quick duck or dive, to emerge on the other side.

Flowstone: A continuous sheet of calcite, covering a cave wall or floor.

Fluorescein: A harmless green dye, used for tracing underground water and its point of resurgence.

Formation: Any decorative cave deposit, including stalactites, stalagmites and helictites.

Gour: A rimstone pool formed by deposits of calcite.

Helictite: A stalactite displaying erratic or eccentric growth.

Joint: A division, often vertical, through a bed of rock.

Karabiner: A metal snap-link used for fastening ropes.

Lifeline: A safety rope, to protect a caver on vertical sections underground

Lycopodium: Spores produced by the lycopodium fern may be dyed and used in water-tracing experiments.

Phreatic cave: A cave formed below the water-table

Pitch: A vertical section of cave, usually requiring the used of a ladder or rope.

Pothole: A vertical shaft, either open to the sky or inside a cave

Resurgence: The point at which underground water emerges at the surface, as in a spring.

Rimstone pool: A small basin with a calcareous edge formed by thin films of flowing water depositing calcite.

Rising: A point where underground water rises to the surface.

Shaft: The vertical entrance to a mine or pothole.

Sinkhole: A place where water sinks or previously disappeared underground

Siphon: A place in a cave passage which is normally totally flooded.

Speleology: The exploration and scientific study of caves.

Squeeze: A narrow place just large enough for a human body to wriggle through.

Stalactite: A formation, usually of calcite, hanging from a cave roof.

Stalagmite: A formation projecting upwards from the floor of a cave.

Strike: An imaginary horizontal line along a bedding plane, at right angles to the true dip.

Sump: A point in a cave where water prevents further exploration, often located at the end of a cave. Short sumps can be negotiated by holding one's breath; longer sumps may be negotiated with the aid of specialist diving equipment.

Swallet: An opening in limestone where a stream vanishes underground.

Swallow hole: An opening through which a stream flows underground.

Water-table: The upper surface of waterlogged rocks or unconsolidated deposits. The phreatic zone lies below the water-table.

INDEX